Table of Revisions/Changes

SECNAV Manual	Basic Issuance Date
SECNAV M-5239.2	May 2009

Change Number	Revision Date

FOREWORD

Cyberspace is the interdependent network of information technology (IT) infrastructures and includes the Internet, telecommunication networks, computer systems, and embedded processors and controllers. Successful cyberspace operations, to include operating, defending, and securing the network, ensure cross-domain freedom of action to our operating forces and the ability to deny that same freedom to our adversaries. The capability to know what is normal and what is abnormal in a dynamic environment of intrusions, viruses, and malware is a competence that must be mastered. In the network domain, the most difficult operational issue will be to fight through a cyber attack. No defense is perfect, and the government will be attacked. The manner in which our Civilians, Officers, Sailors, and Marines fight through these attacks will be vital to our success on the battlefield. No other domain so clearly highlights the intersection of traditional defense, offense, intelligence, counter-intelligence, social interaction, infrastructure performance, military operations, business, and national security constructs. Today's cybersecurity challenges require our people to be skilled, experienced, and given the right tools.

The Department of the Navy (DON) is responding to the immediacy of the cyber threat by increasing Information Assurance (IA) professional workforce training standards. Proper implementation of these guiding policies requires a transformation in DON IA workforce (IAWF) management. This manual sets enterprise parameters for improving workforce policy, processes, and tools to shape the DON's IAWF.

This manual, issued under the authority of the Secretary of the Navy (SECNAV) Instruction (SECNAVINST) 5239.3A, *Department of the Navy Information Assurance Policy,* 20 December 2004, is intended to serve as a high-level policy for IAWF management and is effective immediately.

Robert Carey
Department of the Navy
Chief Information Officer

This page intentionally blank

This page intentionally blank

TABLE OF CONTENTS

1. INTRODUCTION

1.1. PURPOSE

The primary documents that provide direction for this Secretary of the Navy (SECNAV) manual are Department of Defense (DoD) Directive 8570.1, "Information Assurance Training, Certification, and Workforce Management" (reference (a)) and DoD 8570.01 Manual, "Information Assurance Workforce Improvement Program" (reference (b)). This SECNAV manual must be used in conjunction with reference (b) as it does not repeat the detailed levels and functions in the DoD manual. References (c) through (pp) pertain to Information Assurance Workforce (IAWF) management guidance and are contained in Appendix A.

This manual:

1.1.1. Describes Department of the Navy (DON) IAWF management plans and provides direction for implementation of references (a) and (b);

1.1.2. Supplements reference (b) as guidance for the identification and categorization of positions and certification of personnel performing Information Assurance Management (IAM); Information Assurance Technical (IAT); Computer Network Defense Service Provider (CND SP); Information Assurance System Architect and Engineer (IASAE); Certification and Accreditation (C&A); and other IA functions within the DON;

1.1.3. Establishes DON IAWF oversight and management reporting requirements to support implementation of reference (a); and

1.1.4. Establishes IA awareness requirements for information system (IS) users per references (b), (c), and (d).

1.2. OBJECTIVE

1.2.1. Navy and Marine Corps IA Workforce Improvement Program (IA WIP) Office of Primary Responsibility (OPR) will coordinate the implementation and sustainment requirements of this manual to include supporting tools and resources (e.g., conferences, website, database integration, workforce identification); and

1.2.2. This manual will be used for development and execution of Service IAWF Management implementation plans. The requirements and references listed in this manual may be addressed in Service plans.

1.3. APPLICABILITY

1.3.1. This manual applies to DON military (active and reserve), civilian, and contract personnel who work to secure and support the DoD and DON-owned or controlled ISs. It applies to the DON IAWF and their leadership who support classified collateral, and/or sensitive information, or unclassified information systems and networks;

1.3.2. All automated IS users and IAWF members are required to be trained and/or commercially certified. This requirement applies to users of: the Navy Marine Corps Intranet (NMCI); Marine Corps Enterprise Network (MCEN); Overseas Naval Enterprise Network (ONE-NET); Integrated Shipboard Network System (ISNS); Next Generation Enterprise Network (NGEN); Consolidated Afloat Networks and Enterprise Services (CANES); any Program of Record (POR); Research, Development, Test, and Evaluation (RDT&E) systems; or any other approved DON system/network.

1.4. GUIDING PRINCIPLES

The DON's IAWF management strategy is supported by five guiding principles. These principles shape the approach and serve as overarching guidance for implementation of references (a) through (e);

1.4.1. Workforce Skill Consistency. Training and certification will be standardized across the DON to provide the necessary consistency among military, civilian, and contractor job roles and responsibilities to ensure interoperability of all segments of the IAWF;

1.4.2. Total Force Management. Information Assurance is the responsibility of every person in the Department with access to ISs, whether military, civilian, or contractor. Every member of the DON team must be sufficiently trained and aware of IA practices and priorities;

1.4.3. Optimal Enterprise Solutions. DON leadership must pursue enterprise solutions that capitalize on lessons learned and best practices, eliminate redundancy, and ensure the best use of limited resources to achieve significant Department-wide cost efficiencies;

1.4.4. Enforcement of Laws and Regulations. It is crucial that DON personnel protect its Information Technology (IT) infrastructure and the security and privacy of information flowing throughout it. Recent statutory and regulatory guidance to strengthen DON information assurance posture must be adhered to throughout the organization; and

1.4.5. Integration and Alignment. The complexity of this effort demands attention from organizations across the Department, not limited to the functional area of IT, but also including those who shape policy, resources, and databases for management of manpower, personnel, or training.

1.5. GOALS

The goal of this manual is to assist DON leadership and IAWF management by providing guidance that describes desired departmental outcomes and identifies how they will be achieved and measured. For our commands this manual will help strengthen alignment to DON IAWF management priorities.

1.5.1. Manpower, personnel, and training requirements described in this manual must be addressed in the Navy's and Marine Corps' budgets for Fiscal Year (FY) 2010 and beyond per reference (b);

1.5.2. The Services will develop training to support individual competencies required to perform the functions described in references (b), (d), (t), and (u). This is in addition to the baseline commercial certifications;

1.5.3. IAWF advancement, pay, entitlement or career milestones must be considered in individual community manpower and personnel decisions;

1.5.4. Command cultural change is required to improve the command's ability to defend the Global Information Grid. It is essential that personnel who have been trained and certified for specific IAWF billets are assigned to those billets and commanders refrain from assigning those personnel to non IA positions. Conversely, personnel not trained or certified should not be assigned to IA positions;

1.5.5. Standardized IAWF Mission Essential Tasks List (METL) and readiness assessments will be documented in the Defense Readiness Reporting System (DRRS), as mandated by reference (l) for use by the Fleet and Operating Force; and

1.5.6. Future DoD and DON manpower and personnel systems will support integrated personnel and pay processes within the Navy and the Marine Corps, respectively. Additionally, manpower, personnel, training and education tasks will utilize the best IT capabilities available.

1.5.7. The Services will develop individual unit IAWF Management Plans.

1.6. <u>GOVERNANCE</u>

1.6.1. DON IT Workforce governance is depicted in Figure 1 per references (f), (g), (h), (i), (m), (o), (w), (x), (z) and (kk). The DON Chief Information Officer (DON CIO) hosts the Information Executive Council (IEC) with DON Deputy CIO (Navy), (OPNAV-N6) and DON Deputy CIO (Marine Corps) (HQMC C4) as senior oversight board members;

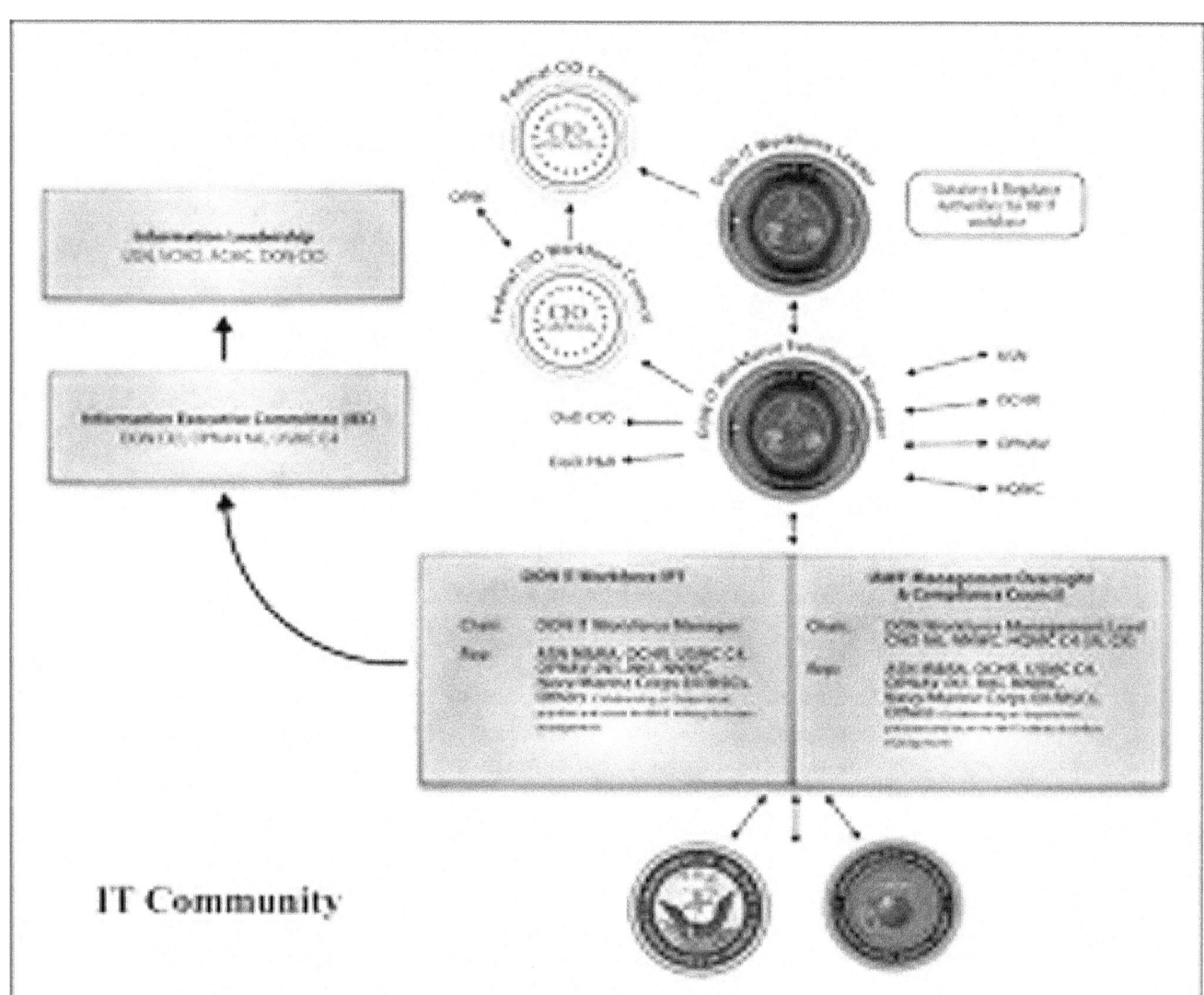

Figure 1: DON IT Workforce Governance Structure

1.6.2. The IAWF Management Oversight and Compliance Council (IAWF MOCC) replaces the Information Assurance Workforce Working Group (IAWWG) established to develop policy, plans, and procedures for implementation of reference (a) requirements. Chartered by reference (z), the IAWF MOCC reports to the Information Executive Council (IEC). The MOCC is lead by an Executive Board comprised of DON CIO, DON Deputy CIO (Navy) and DON Deputy CIO (Marine Corps) and NAVNETWARCOM representatives. This Board is chartered to ensure Service compliance with the IA WIP;

1.6.3. The DON IA WIP must be realized through a standardized, disciplined, and integrated approach that pulls together strategic planning, policy, and resources. Since the IAWF may reside in any shore facility, supporting establishment, operating force, undersea or afloat command, an Enterprise team must be sustained to ensure consistency in implementation of the program in the coming years. Business practices, frameworks, and methods that are aligned across the DON are integral to the implementation of an Enterprise wide IAWF management solution; and

1.6.4. Deputy Chief of Naval Operations (DCNO) Total Force Command and Deputy Commandant Manpower and Reserve Affairs (DC M&RA) functional Office of Primary Responsibility (OPR) shall coordinate with the core IT/C4 communities, as well as the intelligence, logistics, aviation, submarine, and other communities regarding development of proper IAWF management processes and systems as well as funding to support these workforce management tools. Workforce management tools to track positions, personnel, and commercial certifications are a DoD mandate. Strong governance will be required in the following areas:

- Policy and Planning
- Strategic Communications
- Enterprise Requirements Management
- Programming and Budgeting
- Ashore/Afloat/Operating Force/Supporting Establishment Implementation

1.7. IA WORKFORCE MISSION

1.7.1. The cybersecurity mission of the IAWF is to provide security and mission assurance for the interdependent network of IT infrastructures, which include the Internet, telecommunication networks, computer systems, and embedded processors and controllers per reference (c). IAWF functions focus on the design, development, accreditation, configuration, operation, management, and enforcement of security capabilities for systems and networks. Personnel performing IA functions establish IA policies and implement security measures and procedures for affiliated ISs and networks. Per reference (b) descriptions of the IAWF functions are summarized in the following table;

Designated Accrediting Authority (DAA) Functions	Information Assurance Management (IAM) Levels I, II, III	Information Assurance Technical (IAT) Levels I, II, III
Authorize connection/testing Accredit System Authorize IA Controls Accept Risk	Oversee configuration testing Oversee System Revalidate IA Controls Manage Risk	Manage connections/conduct testing Administer System Manage IA Controls Operate (in) Risk
Information Assurance Systems Architects and Engineers (IASAE) Level I, II, III	Computer Network Defense Service Provider (CND SP) Functions	Certification and Accreditation (C&A) Functions
Develop System Design IA Controls Engineer (out) Risk	Monitor System Assess IA Controls Detect Threat	Identify Risk/Audit Certify Recommend Accreditation

Table 1. IA Functional Requirements

1.7.2. To properly execute the IA mission, IAWF management should minimize the number of personnel performing IA duties as a collateral/embedded duty and reduce the number of personnel with privileged network access. Workforce managers should consolidate performance of IA tasks to positions that require personnel to perform IA duties as their primary responsibility. The intention is not to reduce total force numbers but to ensure that personnel performing IA functions are sufficiently trained and certified to do the work. Managers shall strive to concentrate IA functions/job tasks in positions where primary duty is IA functional accomplishment. These actions should begin standardizing the work and reducing the manpower required to accomplish the IA task and professionalize the IAWF.

1.8. IA WORKFORCE STRUCTURE

Commanders/Commanding Officers, in conjunction with the DAA, may designate job titles for the workforce that are appropriate to their job tasks. The complexity of the IT systems, the scope of the work, the operational or experimental nature of the networks, and the knowledge required will drive the grade level of the individual. Position-by-position classification will be based on assigned duties and responsibilities. The same function at activities with different missions may have different grades. The tactical and military operation may be accomplished by a more junior, yet highly trained, workforce member. The positions described below may be considered standards for commands to review when deciding the appropriate manpower requirement. Per reference (d), all IA-related positions are assigned in writing and include a statement of IA responsibilities. Some standard titles are:

1.8.1. Designated Accrediting Authority (DAA). The DAA is the official who formally assumes responsibility for operating a system at an acceptable level of risk. The DAA position shall not be performed by contractors. The enterprise or operational DAA will have significant experience and normally hold the 2210 civilian series National Security Personnel System (NSPS) Security specialty at the GS 15 level (or equivalent). The Developmental DAA will normally hold the 1550, 0854, or 0855 series at the same level. Per reference (y), the DAA position is designated as information security I (IT-I). The DAA must complete DAA training per reference (b) for the following positions.

- Enterprise DAA (USMC)
- Operational DAA (USN)
- Developmental DAA
- Deployed DAA

1.8.2. IA Program Manager. The IA Program Manager (IAPM) is responsible for the business process and controls the funding for the system within a headquarters, acquisition, Navy Echelon II (EII) or Marine Corps Major Subordinate Command (MSC) site, system, or enclave. The IAPM is accountable for the effectiveness of the program and at commands with multiple IAMs; the IAPM may be the senior IAM. The IAPM holds a military designated rank or grade level comparable to the GS 13-15 level (or equivalent) and an information security position designated as IT-I. He/she must have Information Assurance Management level III (IAM level III) commercial certification and an in-depth IT background. A contractor will not hold the IAPM position;

1.8.3. Command Information Officers. All Navy EII Commands and all Marine Corps MSCs shall have a Command Information Officer (Command IO) billet (reference (mm)). Navy EII Command IOs report to the DON Deputy CIO (Navy) for administrative matters and to their Commanding Officer for tactical matters. Marine Corps Command IOs report to both the DON Deputy CIO (Marine Corps) and their MSC per reference (ll). Command IOs hold a position designated as IT-I. Command IOs, normally military 05 or above or civilian equivalent, should take an executive level IA education or training course. A contractor will not hold the Command IO position;

1.8.4. Information Assurance Manager (IAM). The IAM is responsible for ensuring the information system (IS) is operated, used, maintained, and disposed of in accordance with security policies and practices. A sample IAM appointment letter is provided at Appendix C;

1.8.4.1. The IAM fulfilling the functions at the enclave level is expected to have significant IA experience and is responsible to both the local Commander and DAA for ensuring the security of an IS enclave. The IAM will normally be military designated or GS 13-15 (or equivalent). This position may be subordinate to the IAPM or it may be the alternate IAPM. This position could be designated as both the IAPM and IAM depending on the size of the command. It is recommended that this position be filled by personnel in the 2210 series with Security specialty or an officer with an IA specialty or subspecialties. IAMs at the enclave level are designated as IT-I security position and are required to have IAM training level III certification. A contractor will not hold this position;

1.8.4.2. The IAM, fulfilling duties at the network level, reports to the IAM at the enclave, or IAPM, except when there is a single network, in which case he/she reports to the local Commander and Service DAA. The network level IAM position, normally filled by a GS 11-14 (or equivalent) level employee or officer with significant security experience, is responsible for the IA program at the network level. Tactical/shipboard personnel trained to IAM Level II hold a trusted position and rank equivalent to the operational environment, normally staff Non-Commissioned Officer or Chief Petty Officer. Commands with more than one network may have more than one person conducting IAM level II functions; Commands that have more than one network and choose to have separate personnel fulfilling IAM level II functions shall designate one IAM as the command IAM and all others as personnel fulfilling network IAM responsibilities as an information assurance officer (IAO) (see Chapter 1.8.6). IAOs report to the command IAM. Network level IAM positions must meet IT-I security requirements. All personnel fulfilling network IAM functions described in reference (b) shall be required to be trained and certified to meet IAM level II requirements. A contractor will not fill this position, except on a temporary basis with waiver (See waivers in Chapter 4); and

1.8.4.3. The IAM, fulfilling duties at the computing level, reports to the Network IAM within a command, site, system, or enclave. Some IAMs are responsible for the IA program within a command that does not own or host a system or network. In this case, the IAM reports to the local Commander and DAA. In a shore command under the NMCI/NGEN structure (without a network) the IAM may be primarily engaged in training oversight and IS user compliance. If the command has fewer than 25 employees or has a Very Small Site Designation (VSSD), the functions of this job may be performed by a higher level authority with a Memorandum of Agreement (MOA). This is the only IAM job that may be performed on a collateral duty basis. IAMs will be designated IT-II security position and are required to have IAM training level I certification. Contractors may hold this position at level 1.

1.8.5. Certification & Accreditation (C&A). C&A personnel perform tasks required to analyze, assess, and document IA capabilities and services of DoD ISs to establish compliance with IA requirements, identify vulnerabilities, and quantify risk per reference (n). Command C&A personnel provide higher-level authorities such as DAAs and Certifying Authorities with the information needed to make or recommend an accreditation decision. These tasks are normally associated with an established IA C&A process, but may also be performed as part of other related processes or functions. The Services will determine commercial certification requirements for those C&A positions not specified below;

1.8.5.1. Certifying Authority. The Certifying Authority (CA) is the official responsible for performing the comprehensive evaluation of the technical and non-technical security features and safeguards of an IT system, application, or network. In the case of the Marine Corps, the DAA also performs the function of the CA. In the Navy the CA function has been delegated to Space and Naval Warfare Systems Command (SPAWAR). The CA, a government employee, will normally be a GS 15 (or equivalent) level civilian employee. CAs will have significant IA experience and must complete the DAA training as well as IAM level III certification. A contractor will not hold this position;

1.8.5.2. Certifying Authority Representative. The Marine Corps Certifying Authority Representative (CAR) acts as the accreditation representative on the local level and approves all C&A packages that go to the Marine Corps Enterprise DAA/CA. The CAR will have experience and normally hold the 2210 civilian series or a military 06XX Occupation Field designation. CARs must complete the DAA training and IAM level II certification. Contractors will not hold this position;

1.8.5.3. Certifying Authority Leads. The Navy Certifying Authority Leads (CA Leads) act as the accreditation representative for specific systems and approves all C&A packages that go to the Navy CA. The CA Lead will have extensive IA experience and normally hold the 2210, 0854, or 1550 civilian series or a military 16xx, 6xxx, or 7xxx Officer designation. CA Leads must complete the DAA training and IAM level II certification. Contractors will not hold this position; and

1.8.5.4. Validator. The Validator acts on behalf of the Certifying Authority for the C&A testing of IT systems and networks and provides significant input into the production and approval of C&A packages that will be submitted for C&A. Validators will have IAM level II certification. Other individuals that support the Validator in development of the C&A package will have either Information Assurance Technical (IAT) or IAM certification depending on their job functions. Contractors may hold this position.

1.8.6. IA Officers. IA Officers (IAOs) are responsible to an IAM for ensuring the appropriate operational IA posture is maintained for a command, organization, site, or system. If supporting an EII, MSC, or enclave, the IAO will hold positions that meet IT-I or IT-II security requirements and normally hold the 2210 civilian series comparable to a GS 09-14 (or equivalent) or military rank determined by the operational environment, and have IAM level II or III training and certification. They implement and enforce system-level IA controls in accordance with program and policy guidance. The IAO will train and certify to the corresponding level of responsibility stated in appointing letter. Duties of the IAO may be at an IAT or IAM level. A contractor will not perform oversight functions at the Level III environment;

1.8.7. Computer Network Defense-Service Provider (CND SP) Specialty. Personnel assigned as accredited CND-SPs may occupy a position corresponding to a single CND-SP specialty, but they may also perform functions in more than one CND-SP specialty. CND-SP specialty personnel must be fully trained and certified prior to deployment to a combat environment. United States Strategic Command (USSTRATCOM) may approve a waiver for exceptions. CND-SP specialty personnel must have the appropriate baseline IAT or IAM certification training and other training as directed in reference (t). Areas of expertise for the CND-SP specialties include: Infrastructure Support, Incident Management, and Vulnerability Management. IAWF structure titles in the CND SP specialty include:

1.8.7.1. Incident Management/Incident Response. These personnel investigate and analyze activities related to cyber incidents within the network environment (NE) or Enclave. IAT-I or II, CND Incident Responder (CND-IR), and Operating System (OS) certification are required per reference (b). Contractors may perform IM/IR functions;

1.8.7.2. Incident Management /Senior Analyst. Senior personnel investigate and analyze activities related to cyber incidents within the NE or Enclave. IAT- III, CND Incident Responder (CND-IR), and OS certification are required per reference (b). Contractors may perform IM/SA functions;

1.8.7.3. Incident Management/Watch Analyst. These personnel use data collected from a variety of CND tools to analyze events. In addition to the CND Analyst (CND-A) approved commercial certification, Watch Analysts must also gain IAT-I or II and OS certification per reference (b). Contractors may perform IM/WA functions;

1.8.7.4. Infrastructure Support/Sensor Grid Support. These personnel test, implement, deploy, maintain, and administer the infrastructure systems that manage the CND network. IAT-I or II, CND Infrastructure Support (CND-IS), and OS certification are required. Contractors may perform IS/SGS functions;

1.8.7.5. Infrastructure Support. These personnel test, implement, deploy, maintain, and administer the infrastructure systems that manage the CND network. IAT-I or II Certification, CND Infrastructure Support (CND-IS) certification, and OS certification are required. Contractors may perform IS functions;

1.8.7.6. Vulnerability Management Team. These personnel oversee the CND-SP operations. IAM-I or II Certification and CND-SP Manager (CND-SPM) certification are required. Contractors may not hold the CND-SPM position except with a waiver;

1.8.7.7. Red Team. A red team is a group of professionals employed to model the behavior of an adversary. Team members should have significant experience and will maintain a variety of skills set by the Services. Personnel assess systems and networks within the NE or enclave and identify deviations from acceptable configurations or policy. IAT-I, II, or III and OS Certification are required according to the functions performed. At least one member of the team shall hold CND Auditor (CND-AU) certification per reference (b). Contractors may be part of this team; and

1.8.7.8. Blue Team. The blue team's purpose is to conduct IA assessments on systems and networks, identify potential vulnerabilities, and help remediate identified vulnerabilities. Team members should have significant experience and will maintain a variety of skills set by the Services. IAT-I, II, or III, and OS Certification are required depending on the functions performed. At least one member of the team shall hold CND Auditor (CND-AU) certification per functions of reference (b). Contractors may be part of this team.

1.8.8. IA System Architect and Engineer (IASAE) Specialty. DON IASAE functions are focused primarily at the Echelon II and MSC level to support system acquisition and development. Some job functions may occur in Echelon III commands when acting as the Research, Development Test & Evaluation (RDT&E) IA Architecture or Lead Security Engineer representative for the Echelon-II AQ/Development office. Contractors may perform IASAE functions appropriate to their certification level, but may not be able to perform all IASAE functions. IASAE functions relating to requirements generation and entry of requirements into Statements of Work will normally require government personnel or direct government supervision.

1.8.8.1. Systems Engineer. These professionals carry out duties that involve planning, installation, configuration, testing implementation, and management of ISs. They may or may not be part of the IAWF depending on their "privileged access." Personnel must have IAT level II or III certification unless they are working at the enclave, and then they need to certify to IASAE III specialty per reference (b); and

1.8.8.2. Systems Architect. These professionals design, develop, and/or integrate a DoD IA architecture, system, or system components. Personnel must have IAT level II or III certification unless they are working at the enclave, in which case they need to have IASAE III specialty certification per reference (b).

1.9. <u>IA TECHNICAL PERSONNEL</u>

1.9.1. There are many positions and titles for personnel who are involved in IA functions and responsibilities that are not listed above. A large number of personnel have privileged access and have other titles. Anyone with privileged access as defined below is a part of the IAWF and must meet IAT training and certification standards for both IA and the Computing Environment (CE) for the operating system(s) (OS) and/or security related tools/devices they support per reference (b);

1.9.2. Privileged Access. Individuals who have access to system control, monitoring, or administration functions (e.g., system administrator, system programmer) are said to have "privileged access" and therefore, require training and certification to IA Technical levels I, II, or III depending on the functions they perform. They must also be trained and certified on the OS or CE they are required to maintain. They should be a U.S. citizen and must hold local access approvals commensurate with the level of information processed on the system, network, or enclave. They must have IT-I security designation. A person with privileged access must have a National Agency Check with Inquiries (NACI) and/or an initiated Single Scope Background Investigation (SSBI) per reference (d). A contractor may hold this billet. See Chapter 3.13 for further information on Foreign Nationals' security requirements. The workforce assessment in Appendix (F), determines IAWF inclusion. Some examples of jobs that hold privileged access or require personnel to perform IA functions include; and

1.9.2.1. Help Desk Customer Supervisor. To perform customer support functions, Help Desk personnel are part of the IAWF. The supervisor may perform either IAT level II - III or IAM level I functions. Training and both IA and OS commercial certification are required depending on the tier of responsibilities. Contractors may hold this job;

1.9.2.2. Help Desk Service Technician. System administrators may hold the position of help desk service provider. Training for IAT level I-III are required for help desk tier I, II, and III positions. It is not a requirement for all help desk service providers to receive IAT level I-III certifications. The level of permissions or privileged access depends on the job functions. Favorable NACI is required. Contractors may hold this job;

1.9.2.3. Data Manager. This position involves planning, development, implementation and administration of systems for storage and retrieval of data. IAT level I-III training is required for the data manager. Favorable NACI is required. Contractors may hold this job;

1.9.2.4. System Administrator (SA). System Administrators may work in the computing, network, or enclave environments. System administrators shall meet the training and certification requirements for IAT level I at the computing environment (CE), IAT level II at the network environment (NE), and IAT level III at the enclave environment as specified in reference (b). Favorable NACI as well as the initiation of a SSBI per reference (e) is required for all incumbents of these positions; and

1.9.2.5. System Developer. System Developers work to gather, refine, and verify system requirements. The enterprise System Developer will be responsible for the creation, development, testing, and refinement of product concepts, requirements definition, and development execution and may hold IAM certification. Others performing technical tasks with privileged access will need to have both an IA and CE certification, depending on the functions per reference (b) and the Service requirement. In some cases system developers do not require IAM level training or alternatively do not have privileged access and will not need to obtain a commercial certification. Contractors may hold this position.

1.9.3. Authorized Users. As defined in reference (a), an authorized user is any appropriately cleared individual required to access a DoD IS to carry out or assist in a lawful and authorized governmental function. Users are responsible for the protection of data they create and compliance with IA policy requirements. In order to retain IT system access, all users are required to complete and document initial and annual IA awareness training.

2. ROLES AND RESPONSIBILITIES FOR IA WORKFORCE MANAGEMENT

2.1. INTRODUCTION

The DON CIO develops strategy and policy for the DON IA professional workforce per reference (c). Per reference (e), subject to the authority, direction, and control of the Secretary of Defense and subject to the provisions of Chapter 6 of reference (e), the Secretary of the Navy is responsible for, and has the authority necessary to conduct, all affairs of the DON, including the following functions:

- Recruiting
- Organizing
- Supplying
- Equipping (including research and development)
- Training
- Servicing
- Mobilizing
- Demobilizing
- Administering (including the morale and welfare of personnel)
- Maintaining

Per reference (e), the Chief of Naval Operations (CNO) and the Commandant of the Marine Corps (CMC) transmit the plans and recommendations of their offices to the Secretary and advise the Secretary with regard to such plans and recommendations. After approval of the plans or recommendations by the Secretary, the CNO and CMC act as the agent of the Secretary in implementing them. USSTRATCOM is the operational commander of the IA mission. Members of the IAWF, fulfilling IA functions, may also report to Chairman Joint Chiefs of Staff (CJCS) for joint mission requirements and their individual Service for other IA related missions.

2.2. DON CIO IAWF MANAGEMENT RESPONSIBILITIES

2.2.1. The DON CIO is the IT Community Leader and is responsible for oversight of IAWF Management within the Department. DON CIO is also the lead for departmental compliance with external reporting requirements of reference (c). DON CIO appoints:

- Senior IA Officer (SIAO) for IA;
- SIAO for Computer Network Defense (CND); and
- IT Workforce Management Team Lead

Among other things, these senior officers conduct reviews of the Services' programs and validate compliance with the IAWF management requirements. The reviews will include the following:

- Service implementation and sustainment plans for IAWF identification, training, certification, management, reporting, and documentation requirements.

- Service plans and methodologies to track, monitor, and document completion of IA orientation and training requirements for all network users.

2.3. <u>DON DEPUTY CIO (NAVY) & DON DEPUTY CIO (MARINE CORPS) RESPONSIBILITIES</u>

2.3.1. The DON Deputy CIO (Navy) and DON Deputy CIO (Marine Corps), provide support to the DON CIO in his role as the DON IAWF Leader. They collaborate with the manpower, personnel, and training command Offices of Primary Responsibility (OPRs) in the development of Service unique military and civilian training and career management. Additionally, they ensure the core IAWF training, certification, education, and management requirements are met and consistent with DON direction as follows.

2.3.1.1. Develop a strategy for core IT/C4 community workforce development to include recruit, retain, and develop IA personnel throughout their careers (HQMC C4 for Marine Corps/OPNAV N6 for Navy. OPNAV N6 delegates this responsibility to NNWC for implementation);

2.3.1.2. Provide for and electronically track initial IA orientation and annual awareness training of all authorized users. Annual IA awareness training will be reviewed on a yearly basis for applicability and recommended changes submitted to the DON CIO per reference (b);

2.3.1.3. Identify total force structure/positions performing IA management, IA technical, Computer Network Defense Service Provider, Certification and Accreditation, IA Systems Architect, and IA Systems Engineer functions by DoD Instruction 8570.01-M category, specialty, and level per reference (b);

2.3.1.4. Identify IA functions to be performed by contractors in their statement of work/contract and ensure that all DON contracts, requiring performance of IA functions, include the requirement to report contractor personnel's IA commercial certification status per references (b), (m), (kk) and (pp);

2.3.1.5. Ensure personnel obtain the appropriate background investigation/security clearance per reference (y) prior to granting unsupervised privileged access or management responsibilities to any DON system. Contractors also must meet the security eligibility requirements;

2.3.1.6. Electronically track IA personnel who perform IA functions to ensure that IA positions are staffed with trained and certified personnel;

2.3.1.7. Collect metrics and submit reports to the DON CIO to support planning and analysis of the IAWF and annual Federal Information Security Management Act (FISMA) reporting;

2.3.1.8. Provide oversight and coordination for necessary resourcing and implementation of IAWF management plans and processes;

2.3.1.9. Identify all GS-2210 and other IT series positions/personnel (i.e. 0854, 1550) using the Office of Personnel Management specified parenthetical titles or series. Enter the appropriate parenthetical title or series for both primary and secondary responsibilities into Defense Civilian Personnel Data System (DCPDS) or applicable Non-Appropriated Fund (NAF) manpower system per reference (jj);

2.3.1.10. Ensure IA training meets training standards published by the Committee on National Security Systems (CNSS) per reference (u) and/or the National Institute of Standards and Technology (NIST);

2.3.1.11. Coordinate to ensure appropriate IA content is included in officer accession programs, Flag, Commander/Commanding/Executive Officer (CO/XO), and Warrant Officer (WO) indoctrination, and component professional military education. The training will be developed to provide leadership understanding of the critical importance of cybersecurity to the successful execution of the operational mission; and

2.3.1.12. Coordinate the implementation of the DoD Information Assurance Scholarship Program (IASP) with DON CIO.

2.4. DESIGNATED ACCREDITING AUTHORITY RESPONSIBILITIES

DAAs accredit security postures throughout the system development lifecycle in accordance with risk-management principles. A highly trained IAWF is essential to risk mitigation and therefore, the DAAs work collaboratively to enhance IAWF skills. The Operational DAA, at Naval Network Warfare Command (NNWC), and Enterprise DAA at Headquarters Marine Corps (HQMC), Command, Control, Communication, and Computers (C4) will ensure procedures are established to maintain workforce management, training currency, and standardization. Per references (b) and (w) each DAA shall:

2.4.1. Ensure that all IA-related positions are assigned in writing, to include a statement of IA responsibilities and training requirements per references (b), (d), (m), and (w). Appendix C is a sample IAM appointment letter, but Service DAAs may determine the format. One consolidated letter per individual should suffice, but more than one letter may be issued at the commander's discretion;

2.4.2. Maintain list of all command Information Assurance Managers assigned under their cognizance;

2.4.3. Ensure IAWF performing IA functions obtain/maintain an IA certification corresponding to the highest level function(s) required by their position, and if required, an OS/CE certification; and

2.4.4. Ensure documentation of a professional's level of certification as part of DIACAP controls for a system.

2.5. OPERATIONAL CHAIN OF COMMAND

2.5.1. U.S. Strategic Command (USSTRATCOM)/Joint Task Force-Global Network Operations (JTF GNO) provides the operational direction for the IA and CND SP workforce. However, the services implement the training and career progression of IA, CND SP, and Intelligence professionals to meet DoD 8570.01-M.

2.5.2. The National Security Agency (NSA) and USSTRATCOM provide IAWF planning direction, as well as operational direction, for information systems processing Special Compartmented Information, Cryptographic, Cryptologic, Special Access Program, Single Integrated Operation Plan-Extremely Sensitive Information, or North Atlantic Treaty Organization information and implement the baseline requirement per reference

(b) requirement and add other training and certification requirements as appropriate.

2.6. DCNO, TOTAL FORCE AND DC, MANPOWER AND RESERVE AFFAIRS

Manpower, personnel, and training command leadership, by direction of Assistant Secretary of Defense, Manpower and Reserve Affairs, per references (a) and (ii) shall:

2.6.1. Ensure procedures are in place to support the IAWF management transformation;

2.6.2. Provide oversight and coordination for necessary funding of Navy and Marine Corps manpower, personnel, IA education, training, and awareness activities;

2.6.3. Establish career paths that integrate IA Improvement Program requirements;

2.6.4. Establish IA skills training and certification process and provide guidance to service members on enrollment opportunities necessary to complete credential study courses that are part of their approved educational plan leading to a credential;

2.6.5. Ensure training is job-related, distributed equitably, and that all mandatory credentialing requirements are met;

2.6.6. Support the NNWC and HQMC C4 in the identification of IA manpower structure and personnel;

2.6.7. Implement enterprise IA training, certification, and tracking methodologies; and

2.6.8. Implement enterprise training and awareness materials, content, and products on DON IA policies, concepts, procedures, tools, techniques, and systems for the commands to integrate into their IA training and awareness programs.

2.7. ASSISTANT SECRETARY OF THE NAVY FOR MANPOWER AND RESERVE AFFAIRS ASN (M&RA)

ASN (M&RA) (DASN OCHR) personnel responsible for the management of civilian personnel must work with Service communities of interest and community managers to:

2.7.1. Establish policy to ensure IA civilian personnel understand commercial certification requirements;

2.7.2. Ensure civilian training can be captured electronically through the Defense Civilian Personnel Data System (DCPDS) to ensure accurate reporting to higher authority per references (ii) and (jj); and

2.7.3. Provide an enterprise electronic tool to support daily career/training management.

2.8. <u>DON ACQUISITION COMMUNITY</u>

Systems Commands, Program Executive Offices, and the Acquisition Community are responsible for setting up workforce management processes as well as training personnel under their command that have privileged access or significant IA responsibilities. They will:

2.8.1. Appoint IAPMs or IAMs for IT acquisition systems per reference (m);

2.8.2. Ensure contracts carry the appropriate Defense Federal Acquisition Regulations System (DFARS) clause to reflect the requirements of this manual, relating to contracts and contractors per reference (kk);

2.8.3. Ensure the required IA contractor data is entered into the appropriate data bases as required by reference (b); and

2.8.4. Provide appropriate IA training for personnel within the Defense Acquisition Workforce Improvement Act (DAWIA) community that have privileged access or significant IA Management responsibilities.

2.9. <u>ECHELON II AND MAJOR SUBORDINATE COMMAND RESPONSIBILITIES</u>

EII Commanding Officers and MSC Commanders and Command IOs are responsible for DoD 8570.01-M implementation under their cognizance. The Lead IAM or IA Program Manager is responsible for the IA program for a DON organization or IS. The Lead IAM functions as the focal point on behalf of, and principal advisor for, IA matters to the DAA. The EII/MSC IAM supports IA total force planning and shall:

2.9.1. Establish an administrative reporting chain to ensure the appropriate information is reported to higher authority through the DAA;

2.9.2. Oversee an IA program that provides IA manpower and personnel tracking, IA training objectives and policies, and IA training and certification requirements;

2.9.3. Establish procedures to ensure the Command Training Officer sustains the IA training and certification program by reviewing and endorsing command documentation; and

2.9.4. Provide oversight to ensure proper personnel carry out their IAWF management duties.

2.10. COMMANDERS/COMMANDING OFFICERS/OFFICERS IN CHARGE

Commanders, Commanding Officers (COs), and Officers in Charge (OICs) are responsible for IA training and certification compliance. COs and OICs shall:

2.10.1. Ensure the command has an IA Workforce Improvement Plan (IAWIP) that compels training managers to work with IAMs and IAWF Managers to meet shared IA workforce tracking, training, certification, and reporting responsibilities;

2.10.2. Ensure IAWF individual development plans (IDPs) are created that detail specific IA training and certifications required for compliancy;

2.10.3. Review IA structure of the command and identify appropriate staffing requirements;

2.10.4. Promote the professional development and certification of employees who carry out IA responsibilities;

2.10.5. Stabilize workforce rotation in the workplace so trained IA personnel are assigned to IA jobs commensurate with their certifications;

2.10.6. Ensure all IS users (including contractors) are appropriately trained in accordance with reference (b) to fulfill their IA responsibilities before allowing them system or network access; and

2.10.7. Ensure IA contractor personnel have the appropriate appointment letter, IA certification, background investigation, and are being tracked by the command contracting officer's technical representative in the appropriate data base.

2.11. NAVY AND MARINE CORPS RESERVE (USNR/USMCR) COMMAND

USNR and USMCR commands/units will:

2.11.1. Ensure all IA Reserve Force personnel are identified;

2.11.2. Electronically track all IA billets and personnel;

2.11.3. Ensure all IA Reserve personnel hold the designated IA training and certification;

2.11.4. Implement the IAWF Management Program for the Reserve Force that mirrors the Active Force;

2.11.5. Develop procedures for immediate notification and recall of IA personnel as assigned; and

2.11.6. Ensure all Reserve Force Personnel take the initial and annual DoD IA Awareness course.

2.12. INFORMATION ASSURANCE SERVICING AGREEMENTS

Specified IAWF functions may be performed for other commands via Memoranda of Understanding (MOU) or Memoranda of Agreement (MOA). Moving IAWF duties to another command may allow the embedded IA individual to be relieved of duties that can transfer to a full-time IA professional. Such agreements may also be appropriate in situations where security, economy, and efficiency are considerations, including:

- A command provides IAM services for another command, or the command provides services for a tenant activity;
- A command is located on the premises of another government entity and the host command negotiates an agreement for the host to perform IAM functions;
- A senior in the chain of command performs or delegates certain IAM functions for one or more subordinate commands;
- A command with a particular capability for performing an IA function agrees to perform the function for another; or
- A command is established expressly to provide centralized service.

The agreement shall be specific and clearly define the IA management responsibilities of each participant. The agreement shall include requirements for advising commanding officers of any matter directly affecting the IA integrity of the command.

3. IA WORKFORCE MANAGEMENT

3.1. INTRODUCTION

The IAWF is comprised of personnel from many different series and classifications as shown in Appendix B. Workforce management encompasses all the responsibilities for hiring and maintaining a productive workforce that can meet mission requirements. Applicable definitions and acronyms may be found at Appendices D and E. DON IAWF management objectives are to:

3.1.1. Develop a highly skilled DON IAWF with a common understanding of the cybersecurity concepts, principles, and applications for each DoD category, level, and function to enhance protection and availability of DON information, information systems and networks;

3.1.2. Establish baseline skills among personnel performing IA/CND SP/IASAE/C&A and other IA related functions across the DON Enterprise;

3.1.3. Verify workforce knowledge through standard certification testing;

3.1.4. Ensure IA personnel knowledge remains current by defining continuing education requirements to augment knowledge and skills obtained through experience or formal education; and

3.1.5. Identify all positions and personnel with IA responsibilities, regardless of occupational specialty, or whether the duty is performed as primary or as an additional/embedded duty to ensure effective IAWF management.

3.2. TOTAL FORCE PLANNING

Future DON Total Force Planning and Management (TFPM) will be based on anticipated staffing level needs and competency requirements. IA/CND/IASAE/C&A manpower, personnel, and training redundancies and costs must be assessed in accordance with TFPM processes and must support common process and product integration.

3.2.1. Employment of Total Force (TF) assets to meet global requirements is a DON guideline. Further, integration of the Active and Reserve force capabilities and strengths requires cultural change through integrated processes and education at all levels of the TF;

3.2.2. Implementing a standard IAWF requires the adjustment of organizational structures. If the organization's size is large enough to support multiple personnel, individuals with privileged access should be supervised by IA managers to ensure security process integrity. In the case of Research and Development (R&D) commands, the IA responsibilities may be embedded in R&D work. Therefore, determining R&D personnel who are part of the IAWF is not as readily discernible, but must be identified to meet references (b) and (c) mandates by workforce managers and provided to the Service DAAs through the Service Command IO staffs. The organizational construct and relationships must be detailed in Service implementation plans;

3.2.2.1. Per reference (b), commands should look for ways to reduce the number of people with "privileged access." For instance, the tasks of several developer users who own one or perhaps two applications may be transferred to one "privileged user" overseeing several applications. Once the application is installed developers don't log in with their developer account again, unless to reload or install an update; therefore, these personnel do not need daily "privileged access." Commands may designate one person as the system administrator for the developer/engineer group. The designated individual takes care of all system administrator responsibilities and obtains the required certifications. The rest of the users in the group would be ordinary account holders. In some cases the site may consider a centrally managed group of technicians requiring daily privileged access to manage these systems/applications. This tactic reduces the number of people who require 8570.01 compliant certifications and provides the command a stronger System Administrator group overseeing the systems.

3.2.3. An Enterprise IAWF management plan supports efficient utilization of military, civilian, and contractor personnel. Management consists of the following primary segments:

* Recruiting
* Selection and Classification
* Training and Education
* Distribution and Assignment
* Development and Retention

As the Service IA Community Managers and Occupation Field Sponsors map the IAWF functions designated in reference (b), recruiting goals, classification definitions, training regimes, and assignments will need to be adjusted to meet the DON intent of an improved IAWF;

3.2.4. Reference (a) requires the Services review command size and structures to ensure the IA mission can be accomplished. Therefore, IAWF managers must work with the core and expert (embedded) IT individual community management to execute the role of planning, managing, and allocating people and money to the work that needs to be performed. These community specific manpower and personnel management tasks include, but are not limited to:

- Strength planning
- Individual training
- Personnel assignment
- Personnel readiness
- Manpower management
- Accessions
- Mobilization
- Career Development

3.2.5. The DON will develop a highly visible and understood IA organizational competency framework for all positions, structures, and personnel. The manpower and personnel staffs will develop the mechanisms for comparing positions (work) to individual competencies (resumes). This will provide the capabilities of skill capture, skill and position matching, job selection, and learning and career choice. A career/learning management system will be used to provide the ability to assess career paths, position and personnel matching, and skill gap mitigation. The system must interface with tailored delivery of required skills through training, learning, validation, and career choice. It is only through this interactivity that the DON will be able to implement the DoD vision of a highly skilled IAWF.

3.2.6. The DON will use, to the extent possible, existing personnel/manpower and unit organizational databases to satisfy the requirements outlined in this chapter. DCPDS will be used as the authoritative data source for civilian personnel. The DON is responsible for providing this information for military and contractor members through data systems determined by the Service OPRs. DON will leverage Defense Manpower Data Center (DMDC) provided information on commercial certifications to support development of an integrated picture of the DoD IAWF. As practicable, the DON will use the Total Workforce Management System (TWMS) to capture IAWF information.

3.3. INHERENTLY GOVERNMENTAL (I/G)

3.3.1. The Federal Activity Inventory Reform Act, reference (ee), provides a statutory definition of inherently governmental functions and requires annual inventories of commercial activities;

3.3.2. Due to the fundamental nature of cybersecurity in meeting the DON mission, a sufficient cadre of government personnel will be maintained in each area to ensure the continued effective operations of the Information Technology Infrastructure (ITI) under all conditions of peace, operations other than war, national crisis, and war;

3.3.3. The concept of an IT "inherently governmental function" is a function so intimately related to the public interest as to mandate performance by Government employees, this includes those functions deemed to be mission critical. These functions include those activities that require either the exercise of discretion in applying Government authority, or value judgments in making decisions for the Government. Governmental functions normally fall into two categories: (1) the act of governing and (2) monetary transactions and entitlements. Although the IA function, as a whole, cannot be considered to be solely I/G, many aspects of the function are;

3.3.3.1. Government IA personnel need to identify, approve, and issue the IA vision, mission, goals, objectives, and performance measures. Furthermore, the policy-making aspects of performing the function are considered to be implicit in those functions listed as inherently governmental; in general, this means directing or approving the issuance of enterprise policies related to the planning, management, and use of information and associated information technologies; and

3.3.3.2. The DAA, CA, IAPM, privileged access at level III, IAMs at II, III, CND SP, CNA, C&A, IASAE, and those with significant IA duties, may be considered I/G if the functions are deemed to meet the above criteria. Inherently governmental functions must be decided at the unit level per references (bb) through (dd). It is possible that contractors may perform some elements of the inherently governmental functions, but this will usually be in a supporting or consulting role. Leadership and final approval, as well as ultimate responsibility, rests with government personnel.

3.4. CA FUNCTION CODES

3.4.1. Commercial Activity (CA) Function Codes must be reported on all personnel per reference (ee). The function codes are to be used to identify the type of work performed by activities in the Navy infrastructure and operating forces. Each function includes an alphanumeric code, title, and definition describing the type of work performed. Functional definitions are intended to be comprehensive and mutually exclusive. The DON will use the following CA function codes; and

3.4.1.1. W100 for all headquarters IA personnel; and

3.4.1.2. W410 for all other IA personnel

3.4.2. Full Time Equivalents (FTEs) Reported. The number of IA FTE reported in each command inventory should be consistent with the estimated IA FTE funding levels for each fiscal year. Therefore, all budgeted FTE should be included in agency inventories regardless of personnel status (i.e. Civil Service and Foreign Service). Moreover, IA FTE shall be reported whether the IA FTE is filled, vacant, on a non-reimbursable detail, or on extended leave.

3.5. SECURITY CLEARANCE REQUIREMENTS

Personnel requiring "privileged access" to ISs carry an IT and IT-related security designation for processing information within IT systems. All IA personnel are required to obtain U.S. Government security clearance/eligibility in accordance with reference (d). Reference (y) provides DON personnel security standards. System Administrators/Network Administrators for infrastructure devices, IDSs, routers normally will require a favorable NACI as well as the initiation of a Single Scope Background Investigation (SSBI). IA personnel requiring access to ISs processing classified information to fulfill their duties will possess the required favorable security investigation, security eligibility, formal access approval, and need to know. Personnel, while holding a higher level clearance, will only be cleared commensurate with the level of information processed by the information system(s) for which they are responsible. See Chapter 3.13 for Foreign Nationals' security requirements.

3.6. DIVERSITY

The IAWF managers and leaders will promote and engender a culture that embraces the DON's diversity and enables all uniformed members and civil servants to reach their personal and professional potential. To achieve this, the DON CIO is committed to improving diversity up, down, and across the IA enterprise.

3.7. NON APPROPRIATED FUND ACTIVITIES

Non Appropriated Fund (NAF) instrumentalities are normally staffed solely with civilian employees paid by non-appropriated funds. Procedures contained in this manual are mandatory for NAF activities whether the entity is solely staffed by NAF personnel or partially staffed by civilian personnel paid for by appropriated funds. Navy and Marine Corps commands with NAF personnel will track their IAWF as specified by the Service OPRs.

3.8. ACCOUNTABILITY STANDARDS

3.8.1. Accountability standards provide the structural foundation needed to ensure the IAWF management plan supports mission accomplishment. Accountability consists of tracking, feedback, and evaluation methodologies for the IAWF program. All information will be used to make workforce planning decisions; and

3.8.2. DON will institutionalize leadership participation and oversight, broaden understanding of, and participation in, human capital efforts at all levels, improve the data that monitors and guides progress, including implementation of annual employee surveys, and ensure accountability mechanisms are implemented and utilized as intended. See Chapter 5 for accountability and reporting requirements.

3.9. DON IA COMMUNITY MANAGEMENT

IA Community management provides the structure to develop leaders and ensure the junior workforce is being supervised and mentored. Community management is accomplished by collaboration between numerous manpower, personnel, and training commands. Creation of an IA-empowered workforce is only possible with the full support of individual community organizations that integrate the requirements of reference (b) into their community specific career paths.

3.10. IT PARENT COMMUNITIES OF THE CORE IA WORKFORCE

The majority of the uniformed IAWF fulfills IA tasks while being a core part of the officer (IP/IW/C4) and enlisted (IT/CT/C4) functional communities. These professions have a typical career path moving through proficiency levels (basic, foundational, intermediate, advanced, and expert) as they advance in their career. This advancing career path may be known by other names, such as the IT Training Continuum and IT Roadmap.

3.11. CAREER PATHS

Career paths refer to the ability to: (1) move to more senior positions as experience is gained without moving to different career fields; (2) be compensated according to increased skills, and 3) expect that a particular field will provide for advanced training and increasing opportunities.

3.11.1. Core IT/C4 personnel in certain career paths may be required to obtain commercial certifications regardless of whether they are in an IA position. This will ensure IT skills are consistent and standard to an entire community.

3.11.2. The DON must continue to develop highly specialized cybersecurity career paths so the Department's IA specialists are highly skilled. Creating a cybersecurity career path involves a variety of steps to include minimum entry requirements for IAWF positions, specialized training, and standardized certification testing. Examples of specialized training may include digital forensics, intrusion detection, reverse engineering, vulnerability analysis, computer network defense, and IA management. Reference (b) provides only baseline training and certification requirements. Commanders, as well as IAWF personnel, should expect the workforce to participate in continuous professional education in addition to achieving the baseline requirements; and

3.11.3. Working collaboratively, OCHR, personnel management, and Command IOs must offer maximum flexibility in hiring and retaining employees with specialized cybersecurity skills. Some examples may be hiring and retention bonuses, higher education programs, and exchange programs both within the DON and Industry.

3.12. IA CIVILIAN COMMUNITY MANAGEMENT

3.12.1. DON CIO is the IM/IT Civilian Community Leader, and IA is a subset of that community. The Assistant Secretary of the Navy for Manpower and Reserve Affairs (ASN M&RA) provides enterprise policy for civilian personnel. OPNAV N11 supports the Navy civilian communities of interest and teams with DON CIO to foster IA civilian community health and welfare. HQMC C4 leads the Marine Corps civilian IT Community of Interest;

3.12.2. IAWF personnel may be classified under the Office of Personnel Management (OPM) or National Security Personnel System (NSPS) with a specified parenthetical specialty titles per OPM Job Classification Standard (reference (b));

3.12.3. NSPS provides the means for the Department to be a more competitive and progressive civilian employer. A principal objective of NSPS is to facilitate flexible use of civilians when military essential skills are not needed. Staffing flexibilities provide alternative structuring in the way the Department hires, promotes, and adjusts its workforce size. Personnel in several civilian series or specialties may be working as part of the IAWF. Personnel in the 2210 occupational series will identify one parenthetical specialty area, but not more than two specialties. One of the two specialties should be identified as security, if possible;

3.12.3.1. Personnel who perform IA management-related duties would typically be identified as security, project management, or policy and planning in their NSPS parenthetical specialty title. Personnel who perform IA technical-related duties can be identified in any of the following parenthetical specialty titles: applications software, systems administration, operating systems, data management, network services, Internet, systems analysis, or customer support; and

3.12.3.2. Special requirements of the positions, such as security eligibility, travel requirements, etc., should be included under NSPS Position Description DD Form 2918, Block 33, Conditions of Appointment. For IA positions, the following may be used to document the IA position requirement: (1) Position requires IA Category and Level _____ (found in reference (b));or (2) Employee shall obtain and maintain the proper IA certification for information assurance position as required in the DoD 8570.1-M. Upon request of the IAM, the employee shall provide documentation supporting the information assurance certification status. The employee and his or her supervisor shall ensure the employee maintains certification status.

Certification and maintenance requirement for the certification shall be at no cost to the employee. Certified IA personnel performing IA functions whose certification lapses shall have their access to DoD information systems either downgraded to a level appropriate for their certification status or denied access to DoD information systems. Personnel must allow commercial certification providers to report their certification status to the DON.

3.12.3.3. Guidance for writing NSPS Position Descriptions for 1550 and 2210 Series, per references (gg) and (hh), may be found on the DON CIO website (http://www.doncio.navy.mil). The position descriptions can also be used for personnel in other staffing plans.

3.12.4. Direct-Hire Authorities:

Because some IA positions are considered to be critical fills, OPM has authorized the use of direct hire positions. See reference (ff) and consult with your Human Resources Officer regarding direct hire positions. Using OPM-approved government-wide direct-hire authorities, the Services may appoint candidates to IAWF positions without regard to the requirements in title 5 U.S.C. 3309 through 3318. When using the direct-hire authority, the Services must adhere to the public notice requirements in 5 U.S.C. 3327 and 3330, and the displaced employee procedures in 5 CFR part 330, subparts B, F, and G. When documenting appointments using a direct-hire authority, an agency must use two authority codes. The first code is "AYM" and will automatically fill in with "Reg. 337.201." The second authority code will be the individual one associated with the specific direct-hire authority. Information Technology Management (Information Security), GS-2210, GS-9 and above at all locations (GW002, issued June 20, 2003), Second authority Code: BAC.

3.12.5. IAWF Commercial Certification for Civilian Personnel

3.12.5.1. The best course of action to ensure proper enforcement of civilian IAWF commercial certification requirements is to ensure there is proper counseling and documentation. Supervisors should determine how long the person has been in the DON IAWF and fulfilling tasks per reference (b) and mark at least one of the questions noted in appendix (f). If he/she was in a position with "privileged access" or significant IA duties in December 2006, they have until the end of calendar year 2010 to comply with reference b. Personnel fulfilling Information Assurance System Architecture and Engineering (IASAE) and Computer Network Defense Service Provider (CND SP) functions have until 2011. Employees newly hired and placed in a position with certification requirements have six months to obtain commercial certification. Civilian personnel managers and supervisors must ensure:

1. The position description (PD) and the HR hiring checklist contain the requirement to obtain commercial certification as a condition of employment;
2. If necessary the Commanding Officer's appointment letter states that a commercial certification is required to meet DoD Instruction 8570.01-M requirements. See appendix C;
3. Those with "privileged access" should acknowledge the IA and CE commercial certification requirements;
4. The commercial certification process is provided and direction given for the IAWF member to take a commercial certification pre-test, e-Learning, or VTE, and/or classroom training;
5. The command offers remedial training if testing is unsuccessful;
6. The supervisor mentors throughout the commercial certification process;
7. The command offers an employee the opportunity to take the test three times;
8. The individual's supervisor counsels the individual as appropriate;
9. The supervisor/IA professional meetings are documented; and
10. The employee maintains certification currency in accordance with standard procedure.

In the event an individual assigned to an IAWF position does not meet the commercial certification compliance requirements, per reference (b), and all above steps have been taken, the Command will transfer the employee to a non-IAWF position or terminate employment in accordance with established OCHR guidelines.

3.13. FOREIGN NATIONALS/LOCAL NATIONALS

3.13.1. Per reference (d), Foreign Nationals (FN)/Local Nationals (LNs) are not normally part of the DON IAWF and their employment should be minimized. LNs or FNs may be conditionally assigned to IAM Level I and II but may not be assigned to IAM Level III positions (per Reference (d)). LNs/FNs can, however, be privileged users (e.g., system administrators), only with a direct supervisor who is a U.S. citizen. They can receive IAT level I and II training as part of their system administrator duties, but they will not hold the billet or fill the function of an IAT level III;

3.13.2. LNs and FNs must comply with background investigation requirements in accordance with reference (y). LNs or FNs may be conditionally assigned to IAM or IAO IT security level II per reference (d). Additionally, they must comply with background investigation and waiver requirements in accordance with reference (y). FN/LN access to proprietary or personally identifiable information (PII) information also requires a waiver. DAA approval is required as part of the waiver package; and

3.13.3. When compelling reasons exist to employ non-U.S. citizens in IT positions documentation should be part of the waiver request. Per ref (d) LN/FN hires covered by Status of Forces Agreements (SOFA) require host nation vetting at the equivalent level.

3.14. CONTRACTOR MANAGEMENT

United States contractor personnel accessing information systems must meet applicable training and certification requirements per references (b) and (nn). IA contractor personnel career paths are promoted by individual commercial companies vice the government, therefore, private organizations need to ensure their IAWF meets the credentialing regulations in references (b) and (kk).

3.14.1. The Services must modify existing contracts by the end of FY2010 to specify certification requirements. New contracts must state the contractor personnel will agree as a "condition of employment" to obtain the appropriate certification for the position.

3.14.2. DFARS, reference (kk), addresses certification requirements that apply to contractor personnel who perform information assurance functions for DoD, and must be complied within contracts requiring IT/IS support.

3.14.2.1. For acquisitions that include IA functional services for DoD information systems, or that require appropriately cleared contractor personnel to access a DoD information system to perform contract duties, the requiring activity is responsible for providing to the contracting officer: (1) a list of IA functional responsibilities for DoD information systems by category (e.g., technical or management) and level (e.g., computing environment, network environment, or enclave); and (2) the IA training, certification, certification maintenance, and continuing education or sustainment training required for the IA functional responsibilities.

3.14.2.2. After contract award, the requiring activity is responsible for ensuring that the certifications and certification status of all contractor personnel performing IA functions as described in DoD 8570.01-M, IAWF Improvement Program, are in compliance with this manual and are identified, documented, and tracked.

3.14.2.3. The responsibilities specified in this manual apply to all DoD IA duties supported by a contractor, whether performed full-time or part-time as additional or embedded duties, and when using a DoD contract, or a contract or agreement administered by another agency (e.g., under an interagency agreement).

3.15. NAVY OFFICER AND ENLISTED IA COMMUNITY MANAGEMENT

3.15.1. By delegation from OPNAV N6, NNWC is the community sponsor for the Navy core military IA (Information Professional (IP) and Information System Technician (IT)) communities. The DAA provides oversight to IAWF management with special focus on education and training.

3.15.2. For the most part, Navy active officer and enlisted personnel will fall into IA Management levels I and II and IA Technical levels I and II. A much smaller number of personnel will fall into IAM or IAT level III or CND SP. Only a small number of officers will carry out functions for IASAE. Most C&A functions will be performed by civilians or contractors.

3.15.3. Workforce management is required of all communities to include when IA is performed as an embedded duty. Other supporting commands that will provide manpower, personnel or training expertise are:

- Naval Education and Training Command (to include intelligence, aviation, submarine, combat systems, supply centers of excellence)
- Naval Personnel Command
- Naval Manpower Analysis Command
- Centers of Excellence (Information Dominance, Combat Systems, Submarine, Aviation)

- Naval Reserve Command

3.16. MARINE CORPS OFFICER AND ENLISTED IA COMMUNITY MANAGEMENT

3.16.1. HQMC C4 CR is the Occupational Field Management Office for the Marine Corps military C4 community. The DAA will collaborate with IA community management concerning the education and training of the IA community.

3.16.2. For the most part, Marine Corps active officer and enlisted personnel will fall into IA Management levels I and II, and IA Technical levels I and II. A much smaller number of personnel will fall into IAM or IAT level III, or CND SP. Some specialized officer and enlisted billets will perform functions for IASAE, but IASAE requirements for active duty positions will be limited. Most C&A functions will be performed by civilians or contractors.

3.16.3. Workforce management is required of all communities to include those where IA is performed as an embedded duty. Other supporting commands that will provide manpower, personnel, or training expertise are:

- Marine Corps Manpower and Reserve Affairs
- Marine Corps Combat Development Command
- Marine Corps Training and Education Command (to include intelligence, aviation, logistics, etc. schools)
- Marine Corps Communication-Electronics School
- Marine Corps Communication Training Centers

3.17. RESERVE IA COMMUNITY MANAGEMENT

The IA Reserve Force must be developed to fully support the IA mission in the Active Force. ASN (M&RA) provides oversight for the Reserve Force. Chief of Navy Reserve provides the management and operation of the Navy Reserve Force. Commander Marine Corps Reserve provides the management and operation of the Marine Corps Reserve Force. Reserve officers and enlisted personnel are subject to all IAWF management requirements.

3.18. IA SYSTEMS ARCHITECT AND ENGINEER COMMUNITIES

IA systems architect and engineers carry out duties that involve planning, installation, configuration, testing implementation, and management of ISs. IASAE training requirements for the IA systems architect and engineer community will be minimal. It is not anticipated these communities will change their overall career path. The main requirement is the person designated as the command IASAE obtain commercial certifications as appropriate per reference (b), and be tracked per reference (c).

3.18.1. DON usage of the term "integration" for IASAE within Reference (b) Change-1, ought to be viewed as it applies to Design/Development/Demonstration versus production and implementation of ISs. When IS production/implementation is reached, DON IA Architecture and Security Engineer billets will typically be designated at appropriate levels as IAT and IAM requirements, not IASAE.

3.18.2. IASAE functions will require involvement in the requirements and capabilities generation process. Security specific requirements must be embedded in capability definitions and requirements generation, as this is critical to ensure material solutions developed by the Systems Commands have Enterprise level IA requirements addressed within their capabilities documents. In cases where an IA engineering team is involved, only the lead engineer or approver billet would require the IASAE designation.

3.18.3. Each of the commands listed below should organize to sustain at least one IASAE level III billet.

- Assistant Secretary of the Navy Research, Development, and Technical Evaluation (RDT&E)
- Bureau of Medicine
- Bureau of Personnel/Naval Education and Training Command
- Commander Naval Air Systems Command
- Commander Naval Facilities Engineering Command
- Commander Naval Installations
- Commander Naval Network Warfare Command/Global Network Operations and Security Center
- Commander Naval Reserve Forces
- Commander Naval Sea Systems Command
- Commander Naval Supply Systems Command
- Commander Space and Naval Warfare Systems Command
- Director, Strategic Systems Project Office
- Headquarters Marine Corps CP Division
- Marine Corps Combat Development Command
- Marine Corps Systems Command
- Marine Corps Tactical Systems Support Agency

- Naval Nuclear Propulsion Program
- Naval Research Laboratory
- Office Naval Intelligence
- Office of Naval Research
- Program Executive Offices (multiple)

4. IA WORKFORCE EDUCATION AND TRAINING CATEGORIES

4.1. INTRODUCTION

The Services man, equip, and train the workforce. Warfighting effectiveness is realized by developing naval professionals who are highly skilled and optimally employed for mission success. Key to an enhanced and agile workforce is training standardization.

4.1.1. To the maximum extent possible, the DON uses enterprise standards and solutions to implement IAWF training. Enterprise training solutions align the IA training available to the military, civilian, and contractor IA/CND workforce; improve the information available for decision-making; and eliminate redundant expenses. Successful implementation of the IA training standards depends on the following:

4.1.1.1. Connectivity to the centralized training environment or Computer Based Training (CBT) availability at deployed sites where required by the training delivery method;

4.1.1.2. Coordination within the Services to ensure readiness for training, proper timing of training events in relation to deployment, and access to training audiences and subject matter experts (SME);

4.1.1.3. Tasks performed in normal operations will not differ from those performed during wartime or under emergency deployment. Command deployment-specific operations may require a quick refresher prior to a rapid deployment; otherwise the IA common body of knowledge will function the same in war and emergency deployment as it does during normal operations;

4.1.1.4. Mission-specific training must be established and maintained to support afloat and operating forces proficiency. Participation in afloat exercises focuses on standard IA practices. Security Assessment Simulations will be incorporated into operational exercises; and

4.1.1.5. Personnel Qualification Standard (PQS), mentorship, On the Job Training (OJT), virtual training, and e-learning courses are enablers to commercial certification. The services host numerous e-learning courses. The foundations trained in these activities support IA professionals in their commercial certification, but also add consistency, standardization, and discipline to mission accomplishment.

4.2. IA TRAINING STANDARDS

4.2.1. The Committee on National Security Standards (CNSS) was established to set standards for National Security Systems. The CNSS Education, Training, and Awareness IPT oversees the development of IA training standards;

4.2.2. IA personnel follow a training progression that supports continual skill development through individual and team proficiency. No one can expect to be fully qualified, proficient, or knowledgeable until they experience a variety of real life situations. Therefore, training must be developed to ensure IA professionals can grow and continue to meet the cybersecurity mission;

4.2.3. CNSS establishes training standards for the IAWF. These standards, along with mission and system specific training requirements, such as the Computer Network Defense Operating System Environment (CND OSE), define IA training. The DON will implement an IA Training Path with baseline skill requirements conforming to CNSSI. Classroom curricula development may use the following CNSS Instructions; and

4.2.3.1. CNSSI 4011 Information Systems Security Professional;

4.2.3.2. CNSSI 4012 Senior Security Manager (DAA);

4.2.3.3. CNSSI 4013 System Administrator (SA);

4.2.3.4. CNSSI 4014 Information Systems Security Officer/Manager;

4.2.3.5. CNSSI 4015 System Certifier; and

4.2.3.6. CNSSI 4016 IA Risk Analyst.

4.2.4. It is intended for specific topics to be addressed over the continuum of training so that as a person grows in his/her career path they will be exposed to the applicable range of CNSSI training.

4.3. QUALIFIED AND PROFICIENT IA PROFESSIONALS

4.3.1. Various audit reports cite "untrained" people as one of the weakest links in efforts to secure systems and networks. The "people factor" - not technology - is key to providing and ensuring an adequate and appropriate level of security. The DON cannot ensure the confidentiality, integrity, and availability of information in today's highly interconnected network without ensuring all people involved in using and managing IT;

1) Understand their IA roles and responsibilities related to the organizational mission;

2) Understand the organization's IA policies, standards, procedures, and practices;

3) Have certifiable knowledge of the various management, operational, and technical controls available and required to protect the IT resources for which they are responsible; and

4) Can easily interchange with other service members and accomplish work as a standard part of the Joint/DoD workforce.

4.3.2. The training continuum or road map provides a guide for professional development throughout the entire career of the DON IA professional. Personnel will commence fundamental/core training at the beginning of their career and advance to networking specific professional education. Supervisors and training officers will use service training plans to support the development of the Individual Development Plans (IDPs) for IT professionals under their supervision;

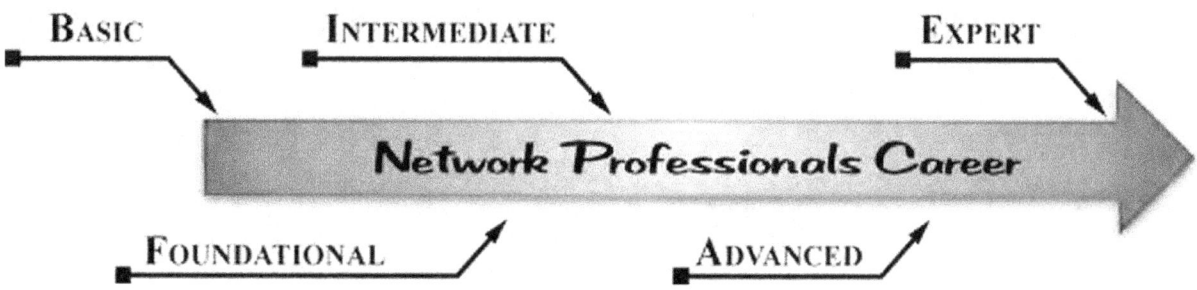

Figure 2: Training Continuum

4.3.3. The DON requires IA professionals to complete a minimum of 40 hours of continuing professional education (CPE) in the IA field. Examples of CPE are;

4.3.3.1. National Defense University/Information Resource Management College INFOSEC Professional, CNSSI 4011;

4.3.3.2. Naval Postgraduate School courses;

4.3.3.3. The Computer Network Defense Operating System Environment (Host Based Security System (HBSS) - McAfee Hercules; Secure Computing Configuration Vulnerability Initiative (SCCVI); Secure Computing Remediation Initiative (SCRI);

4.3.3.4. DIACAP/C&A;

4.3.3.5. Global Information Grid (GIG) policies;

4.3.3.6. OSD policies and procedures;

4.3.3.7. DON Policies and procedures;

4.3.3.8. JTF GNO directives;

4.3.3.9. Other OS/CE certifications, (See Appendix G Guidance);

4.3.3.10. Other fleet tools and applications (training, personnel, management systems);

4.3.3.11. Any service IA or AFCEA conference;

4.3.3.12. Command specific requirements; and

4.3.3.13. On the job training that results in Personal Qualification Standards.

4.3.4. All IA CPE should be documented in each IA professional's IDP; and

4.3.5. IA Professionals are encouraged to matriculate to higher level education. Advanced education enhances the workforce knowledge level while commercial certification testing is a method to ensure workforce knowledge and skills are standardized.

4.4. BLENDED TRAINING SOLUTION

4.4.1. IA personnel will be trained to perform the functions of their assigned position through a blended solution of formal classroom training, experiential activities, electronic training media, and continuing education. Training and certification opportunities will be provided by the DON at no cost to government employees (military or civilian). Enterprise blended solutions will be provided at the most economical cost feasible.

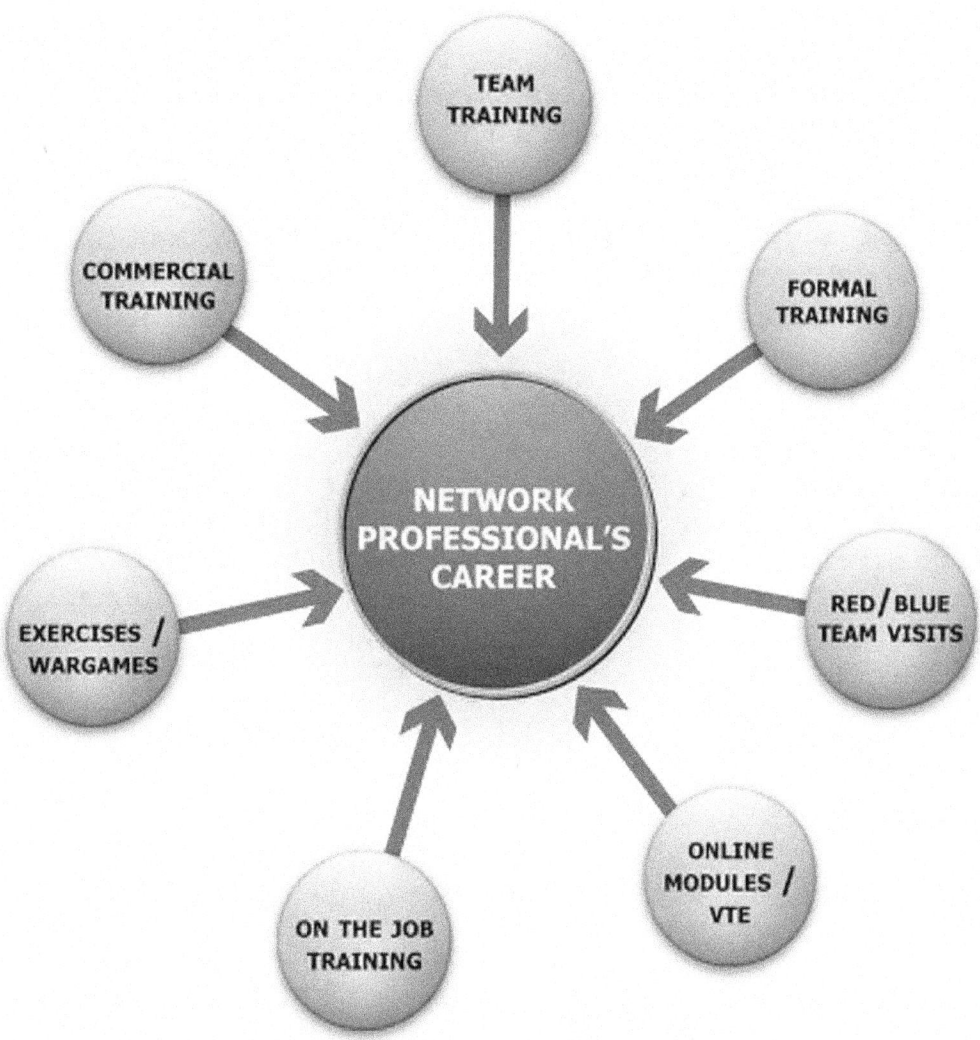

Figure 3: Training and Certification Continuum

4.4.2. The Navy Center for Information Dominance and Marine Corps Communications and Electronic Schools will develop baseline IA training that may be used by IA professionals in intelligence, logistics, aviation, combat systems, and other functional communities.

4.4.3. Education and training will be delivered through a variety of standards based methods. Based upon training requirements, training effectiveness, cost, and individual professional development, delivery methodology may include as part of the standard training continuum: conventional classrooms, mobile training teams, advanced distributed learning, computer based training (CBT), self-paced interactive courseware, simulation/war games/exercises, commercial training/certifications, university/college/service schools, mentoring, on-the-job Training (OJT) and off-site team training.

4.4.4. "Develop once, deliver many times" is a goal that allows the cost of training development to bring a return on investment. IA training is required at some 300 ships and 3,000 Navy and Marine Corps sites around the world, including combat training centers, Command and Control nodes, military task forces, and Joint task forces. Enterprise training, train-the-trainer training, e-learning, virtual training, and instructor-led training serve to both standardize training and minimize training costs.

4.4.5. Modular Design, Development, and Implementation. Personnel from different communities, but with the same job positions or tasks, require the same knowledge, skills, and abilities. Therefore, service schools will employ a modular approach to the design and development of individual lessons. Training curricula will be designed to enable module interchangeability between job classifications. Content domains with similar structure must be identified early in the development process, so the information can be shared across communities. This approach to curriculum design will reduce redundancy in training development.

4.5. COMMERCIAL CERTIFICATIONS

Commercial certifications will provide a standard to measure IAWF baseline knowledge. The DON OPR will coordinate with the commercial vendors to ensure commercial training and certification availability and accessibility adhere to Service operational commitments.

4.5.1. Vendors desiring to support DON reference (b) commercial certification efforts should provide:

4.5.1.1. Electronic testing;

4.5.1.2. Week-day testing;

4.5.1.3. At a minimum monthly testing;

4.5.1.4. Continuous learning model, vice recertification, to keep the information current (proctoring is not considered a valid way to gain Continuing Professional Education (CPEs)); and

4.5.1.5. Cost effective testing.

4.5.2. The Service OPRs will determine the minimum baseline certification requirements for both the IA and CE/OS certifications. Appendix G provides a list of CE/OS certifications for command consideration. Enterprise training costs will be negotiated with individual vendors, therefore, command leadership and personnel should refer to Service requirements prior to engaging in commercial training and certification.

4.5.3. The Services will fund the certification training and certification test voucher required for the specific IAWF position. In the event of a first certification test failure, the DON will fund for two additional tests provided the individual takes remedial training and subsequent electronic pretests to ensure the level of knowledge is addressed. In the event of a third certification test failure, Commanders will determine remedial action, and it may become the individual's responsibility to fund and successfully pass any subsequent certification retest within the mandatory six month window.

4.5.4. Uniformed IA professionals shall have, at a minimum, one year remaining on their enlistment prior to receiving pre-paid vouchers or reimbursement for credentialing/licensing exam, renewal, and maintenance fees authorized by reference (oo). Service members do not sign a continued service obligation for obtaining IA training and certification test vouchers. In all cases, prior to registering/taking an exam or obligating funds out-of-pocket, the Professional Certification and Licensing Voucher Request form must be completed and submitted to receive exam funding or reimbursement authorization.

4.5.5. DoD requires each certified member of the IAWF to authorize the release of their certification status in the Defense Workforce Certification Authorization (DWCA) tool to remain eligible for their current IA position. Additionally, the IAWF will allow their CPEs to be reported to the commercial vendor.

4.6. COMMERCIAL CERTIFICATION VOUCHERS

Command Training Officers/IAMs may request IA commercial certification test vouchers directly through the Personnel Certification Support System (PCSS), an on-line DoD Commercial Certification exam voucher request/distribution application. This DoD application will be hosted on Navy servers and used by the Navy's Credentials Program Office (CPO) as a "paperless" test voucher application tool. The CPO endeavors to provide commercial certification test vouchers to the IA professional within 72 hours of the request. This tool makes the voucher request processing more efficient, accurate, and accessible for users as well as leadership.

4.7. OPERATING SYSTEM CERTIFICATIONS

Operating System and Computing Environment training normally culminates in a standard test and subsequent commercial certification. However, there may be instances of factory training or Systems Command training that result in a certificate. In cases where service mandated training is judged to meet a baseline standard, the System OPR will request exception to the commercial certification requirement to the Service OPRs who will approve the training standard.

4.8. WAIVERS

4.8.1. DAAs may waive the certification requirement under severe operational or personnel constraints. The waiver will be documented by the DAA using a memorandum for the record stating the reason for the waiver and the plan to rectify the constraint. Waivers will not extend beyond six months and consecutive waivers for personnel are not normally authorized.

4.8.2. IA personnel must be fully trained and certified prior to deployment to a combat environment. The DAA may grant an interim waiver limited to the deployment. The waiver must include an expiration date not to exceed six months following return from combat status.

4.8.3. Waiver requests should be forwarded only under severe operational or personnel constraint cases to the Navy and Marine Corps IAWF OPR, who will review them prior to DAA approval.

4.9. SECTION 508

The training products developed to support the IA community will conform to the Rehabilitation Act of 1998 per reference (11), which requires Federal agencies to make their electronic and information technology accessible to people with disabilities. Section 508 was enacted to eliminate barriers in information technology, to make available new opportunities for people with disabilities, and to encourage development of technologies to help achieve these goals. The law applies to all federal agencies when they develop, procure, maintain, or use electronic and information technology.

4.10. ADVANCED EDUCATION

4.10.1. Professional Military Education (PME) should be reviewed to ensure IA awareness and training is incorporated.

4.10.2. Advanced education degrees are encouraged. IAWF personnel holding advanced degrees will still comply with commercial certification requirements to ensure standardization.

4.10.3. The DoD IA Scholarship Program (IASP) is a mechanism for current DoD military and civilian employees to earn a masters and/or PhD degree in an IA related field of study from a university designated by NSA as Centers of Academic Excellence in IA education. The DON will support this program.

4.11. REMEDIAL TRAINING

Remedial training may be required when the individual fails to pass the standard commercial certification test for his position or when the command determines the individual cannot complete his job tasks and functions satisfactorily. Regardless of when remedial training begins, the person must be certified within a six month timeframe from assignment of duties.

4.11.1. Commands should offer focused and goal oriented remedial coaching and training to address the gaps in a person's IA knowledge base. This may be determined by the IA commercial certification pre-assessments taken through the service IA training systems.

4.11.2. After remedial training, individuals in IA positions not meeting certification requirements must be reassigned to other duties, consistent with applicable law. Non-certified personnel may perform those duties under the direct supervision of a certified individual during the 8570.1 implementation phase and no greater then six months for new hires.

4.12. CONTRACTOR PERSONNEL TRAINING

Once the IAWIP is fully implemented, contractor personnel supporting IA functions will normally be appropriately certified prior to being placed on a task. Once the proper documentation is placed in the individual's contract/statement of work, the contracting officer will ensure all contractors are appropriately certified and tracked in the appropriate authoritative DoD system and TWMS.

4.13. <u>LOCAL NATIONAL TRAINING</u>

Organizations employing LNs should coordinate in advance with appropriate offices regarding requirements outlined in the Status of Forces Agreement, the local or country human resources section of OPM, local unions' documentation, and or training documents. Effective coordination will greatly enhance the capability to credential the LN to the appropriate level and achieve the requirements of this manual.

4.14. <u>COMBATANT COMMAND (COCOM) IA TRAINING</u>

4.14.1. Combatant Command government civilians will register and request commercial certification vouchers through the Service Executive Agent (EA) for the COCOM. Combatant Commands that use Navy as the EA need to ensure government civilians positions filling designated (IAT or IAM) are registered in DCPDS, Defense Workforce Certification Application (DWCA) , and request vouchers through the PCSS; and

4.14.2. Military personnel, stationed at COCOMs, will register and request vouchers through their Service system/process. COCOMs need to ensure military personnel filling positions designated (IAT or IAM) are registered in the Electronic Joint Manpower and Personnel System (e-JMAPS) and Service personnel systems as appropriate.

4.15. <u>AUTHORIZED USER AWARENESS REQUIREMENTS</u>

4.15.1. IT users need to maintain a degree of understanding about IA policies and doctrine commensurate with their responsibilities. The focus must be on aspects of IA that impact the authorized user and place particular emphasis on actions the authorized user can take to mitigate threats and vulnerabilities to DoD ISs. Authorized users must understand they are a critical link in their organization's overall IA posture.

4.15.2. DISA's DoD IA Awareness CBT is the DON baseline standard. It meets all DoD level requirements for end user awareness training. DISA will ensure it provides content that enhances awareness to address evolving requirements promulgated by Congress, OMB, or the Office of the Secretary of Defense. DISA's training products can be accessed via the DoD IA portal and Navy and Marine Corps elearning systems.

4.15.3. DON commands are expected to address organization specific topics and local incident reporting procedures by using

IA awareness training (in person or elearning) or other awareness techniques such as posters, email alerts, short movies, or command "tips of the day".

4.16. <u>GENERAL USER TRAINING REQUIREMENTS</u>

4.16.1. All individuals with access to DoD IT systems are required to receive initial IA orientation before being granted access to the system(s) and receive annual IA awareness training to retain access. All users will be informed of their information and IS security responsibilities and consent to monitoring.

4.16.2. At a minimum, the following themes must be conveyed in IA initial orientation and annual awareness programs:

- Critical reliance on information and IS resources.
- Threats, vulnerabilities, and related risks associated with IS.
- Common causes of electronic spillages, as well as ways to prevent/detect the same.
- Consequences for inadequate protection of an organization's IS resources.
- The essential role of the DoD employee in a successful IA program.

4.16.3. Commands must maintain the status of user orientation and awareness compliance. Required versus actual IA orientation and awareness will be a management review item per reference (b) and (c).

5. IA WORKFORCE MANAGEMENT REPORTING AND METRICS

5.1. INTRODUCTION

Measures are used to facilitate decision making and improve performance and accountability through the collection, analysis, and reporting of performance-related data. An effective IA WIP will be created when controls and measurements are put in place. For the IAWF, policies and procedures will be backed by the authority necessary to enforce compliance.

5.2. OVERSIGHT AND COMPLIANCE

5.2.1. DON IAWF management status and accomplishment will be reported to the Assistant Secretary of Defense for Networks and Information Integration/DoD Chief Information Officer (ASD (NII)/DoD CIO) and furthermore, to Congress per references (a) and (c).

5.2.2. The Federal Information Security Management Act of 2002 (FISMA), reference (c), is a part of the E-Government Act of 2002 (PL 107-347). FISMA requires government agencies to improve the security of federal information and information systems.

5.2.3. FISMA requires DoD to report to Congress annually, addressing the adequacy and effectiveness of information security policies, procedures, and practices to include IA training. In addition to the annual report, FISMA requires each agency to conduct an annual independent evaluation of the IA program and practices to determine their effectiveness.

5.3. DOD ANNUAL REPORT

5.3.1. The IA training and certification program annual report to DoD is due at the end of each calendar year and may use the FISMA report, reference (c), as the quantitative part of the report.

5.3.2. ASD NII/ DoD CIO coordinates IA Training and Certification Program reporting requirements, and ensures collected information supports ASD NII/ DoD CIO validation of DoD IAWF readiness. The DON provides both qualitative and quantitative information delineated herein.

5.3.3. DoD Qualitative Requirements. The DON will describe the methodologies, requirements, and processes used to implement the IA WIP. Specifically, DON will report:

- Methodologies used to identify employees in the IAWF;
- Training and certification requirements developed for employees in the IAWF, such as DON schools/training centers, IA related curriculum status, and actual/planned annual throughput;
- Programs to train and certify personnel performing IA functions;
- Methodologies used to track IA orientation and awareness training for all network users;
- Status of recruitment and retention for the IAWF, indicating if it is increasing, stable, or decreasing, and why;
- IA curriculum/treatment in CAPSTONE, officer accession programs, Flag, C.O., Executive Officer, and Warrant Officer indoctrination and PME courses;
- Defense colleges, universities, PME, IA related curriculum, and actual/planned annual throughput;

5.3.4. DoD Quantitative Data Requirements. The Service OPRs will work with the appropriate manpower and personnel OPRs to ensure its personnel and staffing databases are properly configured to electronically, per references (p) through (s), capture the following quantitative data.

- IAWF positions and manning status (this is a management review item);
- Number of IAWF positions, by category and level;
- Number of primary duty IAWF positions;
- Number of additional/embedded duty IAWF positions;
- Number of IAWF positions filled by category and level;
- Number of IAWF positions filled with certified personnel by category and level;
- Personnel certification levels (this is a management review item);
- Number of personnel certified by category and level;
- Number of personnel certified by category and level, who are filling an IA position;
- Recertification rates, number of personnel who were recertified during the current year;
- Total dollars obligated or expended for IA training and certification;
- Compliance with IAWF certification continuing education/sustainment training requirement; and

- Number of users who completed IA orientation and awareness training requirement versus total number of authorized users (this is a management review item)

5.4. COMPLIANCE VISITS

5.4.1. In addition to annual reports, IAWF leadership will use personal verification to ensure compliance. Command IAWF disposition may be reviewed in the following activities.

- Naval Audit Visits
- Inspector General Visits
- Red Team Visits
- Blue Team Assist Visits
- Headquarters level visits

5.4.2. Appendix H is an IAWF management review checklist that activities may use to assess themselves, improve their programs, and prepare for workforce management related visits.

5.5. COMMAND RESPONSIBILITY

Commanding Officers shall establish a unit level IA WIP. The IA WIP will be an inspection item during compliance visits. The central goal of the IA WIP is to better operate and defend DON assets of the GIG. By influencing the Department's workforce, both general users and IT professionals, to change behavior and attitudes, leadership will play a critical role in motivating every employee to do their part in protecting national security while accomplishing the command cybersecurity mission.

5.6. PERSONAL RESPONSIBILITY

All IA professionals must work with their leadership to ensure their own training and education meets national security standards and they are fully commercially certified and have completed OJT and CPEs in accordance with reference (b).

5.7. FUNDING REQUIREMENTS

5.7.1. The services use the Joint Capabilities Integration and Development System (JCIDS) to determine doctrine, organization, training, materiel, leadership and education, personnel and facilities (DOTMLPF). In order to meet future military challenges, the IAWF organization, training, education, and personnel solutions are determined through this process;

5.7.2. DoD provides a phased approach to implement reference (b). The first year provides time for the identification of specific requirements to support budget and staffing planning, and to certify the initial 10 percent of the IAWF. This phased approach provides time to bring the full IAWF into compliance. By FY11 the entire workforce must be in compliance. To support this implementation the Services will budget for IA training, certification, and workforce management requirements, as described below.

- Fund and staff identified IA positions (primary or additional/embedded duty).
- Fund Training and certification for current and future IAWF members.
- Ensure databases/tools are upgraded to support IAWF management requirements.
- Fund training for staffing managers on the systems and processes required to support the IAWF training and management requirements.

5.7.3. Per reference (b) the DON will annually report progress to ASD NII/DoD CIO on budgeting to meet implementation requirements using the format in Figure 4.

IA Workforce Milestone Budget Plans (training and certification, costs)								
IAWF Budget	PY	CY	BY00	BY01	BY02	BY03	BY04	Total
Required								
Budgeted								
Obligated								

Figure 4.   IA Workforce Milestone Budget Plan Report

APPENDIX A - REFERENCES

View http://iase.disa.mil/policy.html for a list of all IA-related laws, regulations, and DoD policies.

a. DoD Directive 8570.1, "Information Assurance Training, Certification, and Workforce Management," 15 Aug 2004.

b. DoD 8570.01-M, "Information Assurance Workforce Improvement Program" of 19 Dec 2005.

c. Section 3544 of Title 44, United States Code (as added by the Federal Information Security Management Act (FISMA) of 2002).

d. DoD Instruction 8500.2, "Information Assurance Implementation," 6 Feb 2003.

e. Title 10, United States Code."

f. Section 278g-3 of Title 15, United States Code, (added by Computer Security Act of 1987).

g. Office of Management and Budget Circular A-130, "Management of Federal Information Resources, Transmittal 4," November 30, 2000, Appendix 3.

h. (HSPD) 23 Homeland Security Presidential Directive on National Cybersecurity Initiative.

i. SECNAVINST 5430.7P, "Assignment of Responsibilities and Authorities in the Office of the Secretary of the Navy", 26 Jun 2008.

j. DoD Directive 8500.01E, "Information Assurance," 24 Oct 2002.

k. DoD Directive O-8530.1 "Computer Network Defense," 8 Jan 2001.

l. DoD Directive 7730.65, "Department of Defense Readiness Reporting System (DRRS)," 03 Jun 2002.

m. DoD Directive 8580.1 "Information Assurance in The Defense Acquisition System," 9 Jul 2004

n. DoD Instruction 8510.01, "DoD Information Assurance Certification and Accreditation Process (DIACAP)", 28 Nov 2007

o. SECNAVINST 5239.3A, "DON IA Policy", of 20 Dec 2004.

p. DoD Instruction 7730.64, "Automated Extracts of Manpower and Unit Organizational Element Files," 11 Dec 2004.

q. DoD I 1336.5, "Automated Extracts of Active Duty Military Personnel Records," 2 May 2001.

r. DoD Instruction 7730.54, "Reserve Components Common Personnel Data System (RCCPDS)," 6 Aug 2004.

s. DoD Instruction 1444.2 "Consolidation of Automated Civilian Personnel Records," 16 Sep 1987.

t. CJCS Manual 6510.01, Defense-in-Depth: Information Assurance (IA) and Computer Network Defense (CND), Current as of 12 Aug 2008

u. CNSSI No. 4011-4016, "National Information Security System Instructions."

v. Title 29, Code of Federal Regulations, section 1607, current edition

w. SECNAV M-5239.1, "DON IA Program, IA Manual," of Nov 2005.

x. DON Information Management and Information Technology Strategic Plan, series.

y. SECNAV M-5510.30, DON Personnel Security Program Manual, 30 Jun 06

z. DON CIO Information Assurance Workforce Management Oversight Charter of 16 Mar 2009.

aa. DoD Instruction 1400.25, "DoD Civilian Personnel Management System: Volume 250, Civilian Strategic Human Capital Planning (SHCP)" Volume 250, 18 Nov 2008.

bb. Public Law 105-270, Federal Activity Inventory Reform Act. "Inherently Governmental Functions."

cc. DON CIO IM/IT Inherently Governmental Guidance, Nov 2001

dd. DoD Directive 1100.4, "Guidance for Manpower Management," 12 Feb 2005.

ee. DOD Instruction 1100.22 , "Guidance for Determining Workforce Mix" of 7 Sep 2006.

ff. Direct-Hire Authorities: 5 U.S.C. Section 3304/5 CFR Part 337, Subpart B, 5 U.S.C. 3309 through 3318. 5 U.S.C. 3327 and 3330, 5 CFR part 330, subparts B, F, and G.

gg. DON Guide for Development of Position Descriptions under National Security Personnel System for the Occupational Code 2210, Information Technology Specialist of 4 Jun 2008.

hh. DON Guide for Development of Position Descriptions under National Security Personnel System for the Occupational Code 1550, Computer Scientist of 25 Sep 2008.

ii. USD P&R, memo, "Human Resources Support to Implementing DoD Information Assurance Workforce Training, Certification and Workforce Management Requirements," of 8 Jan 2007.

jj. USD P&R, memo, Update of Information Assurance (IA) Training and Certification Data in the Defense Civilian Personnel Data System DCPDS, 4 Jun 20007

kk. DoD Acquisition Regulations System (DFARS) 48 CFR Parts 239 and 252 RIN 0750-AF52, Supplement; Information Assurance Contractor Training and Certification (DFARS Case 2006-D023).

ll. DON memorandum to CNO and CMC, "Designation of the Department of the Navy Deputy Chief Information Officer (NAVY) and the Department of the Navy Deputy Chief Information Officer (MARINE CORPS)," 22 Aug 2005.

mm. DON CIO Memo "Roles, relationships and Core Competencies of DON Command Information Officers," 25 Jan 2008

nn. Section 508 (29 U.S.C. 794d) of the Rehabilitation Act of 1998

oo. OPNAVINST 1540.56, "Navy Credentialing Programs," 6 Sep 2007

pp. NISPOM, National Industrial Security Program Operating Man, reissued 28 Feb 2006

APPENDIX B - IA WORKFORCE BY SERIES

Full Time and Embedded IA Personnel: The diverse IAWF consists of both traditional (IT and C4) and non traditional occupational series and ratings. Non appropriated fund and foreign and local national personnel IAWF are also included. The individual service IAWF office of primary responsibility (OPR) will define IAWF positions and personnel. The IAWF includes any uniformed military, civilian, or contractor personnel who have privileged access or major IA management responsibilities. Note, not all personnel holding the below series are in the IAWF, but personnel holding these series have been identified as performing IA functions. Personnel completing reference (b) functions must comply with the stated training and certification requirements regardless of occupational designation. This is not an all inclusive list of series or specialties that carry out IA functions in some 3,000 DON commands.

Civilian Series	Marine Corps Military Occupational Specialty (MOS) (Officer)	Navy Officer Designator	Marine Corps MOS (Enlisted)	Navy Enlisted Classifications (NEC)
0332, 0334, 0335, 0340, 0343, 0390, 0391, 0392, 0394, 0854, 0855, 0856, 1411, 1412, 1421, 1550, 2203, 2204, 2210 2210 Parentheticals: Applications Software Customer Support Data Management Internet Network Services Operating Systems Policy and Planning Project Management Security Systems Administration Systems Analysis	0602, 0603, 0610, 0620, 0640, 0650, 8846, 8055, 8848, 8858	1600, 1610, 1630, 6120, 6190, 6280, 6290, 6420, 6490, 7180, 7190, 7280, 7420, 7490,	0211, 0612, 0619, 0628, 0629, 0231, 0621, 0622, 0623, 0627, 0628, 0651, 0659, 0681, 0689, 2611, 2621, 2621, 2629, 2631, 2651, 2821, 2823, 2847, 2862, 6694, 0699	2709, 2710, 2720, 2730, 2735, 2777, 2778, 2779, 2780, 2781, 2782, 2783, 2301, 2306, 2379, 0469, 0509, 0510, 0522, 0525, 1104, 1136, 1144, 1318, 1331, 1332, 1335, 1336, 14xx, 1493, 1613, 1654, 1678, 9136, 9150, 9605, 9613

APPENDIX C - DON SAMPLE IAM APPOINTMENT LETTER

From: <Commander/Commanding Officer>
To: <IA professional>

Subj: APPOINTMENT OF FIRST M. LAST, AS INFORMATION ASSURANCE
        MANAGER (IAM)

Ref:
    (a) DoD Instruction 8500.1, Information Assurance, 24 Oct
        02
    (b) DoD Instruction 8500.2, Information Assurance (IA)
        Implementation, 6 Feb 03
    (c) DoD Directive 8570.1, "Information Assurance Training,
        Certification, and Workforce Management," 15 Aug 2004
    (d) DoD 8570.01-M, "Information Assurance Workforce
        Improvement Program" of 19 Dec 2005
    (e) SECNAV M-5239.2 DON IA Workforce Management Manual,
        (this manual)
    (f) CJCS Instruction 6510.01D, Information Assurance and
        Computer Network Defense, 15 Jun 04
    (g) CJCS Manual 6510.01, Defense-in-Depth: Information
        Assurance (IA) and Computer Network Defense (CND),
        Current as of 12 Aug 2008
    (h) SECNAVINST 5239.3A, "DON IA Policy", of 20 Dec 2004
    (i) DoD Instruction 8510.01, DoD Information Assurance
        Certification and Accreditation Process (DIACAP)", 28
        Nov 07
    (j) DoD 5200.1-R DoD Information Security Program
        Regulation, Jan 97
    (k) SECNAV M-5510.30, DON Personnel Security Program
        Manual, 30 Jun 06
    (l) SECNAV M-5510.36 DON Information Security Program (ISP)
        Regulation, 30 Jun 06
    (m) SECNAV M-5239.2, DON IA Workforce Management Manual, 29
        May 2009

1. In compliance with requirements set forth in references (a)
through (e), and additional IAM functions outlined in references
(f) through (m), you are hereby appointed as the Information
Assurance Manager (IAM) for (COMMAND). As the primary IA
advisor, you will report to and advise me on all IA issues for
all unclassified systems and networks within (COMMAND).

2. You are required to comply with the security requirements of
reference (j) through (l), and hold a U.S. Government security

clearance commensurate with the level of information processed by the information system(s) for which you are responsible.

3. Your duties as the IAM include, but are not limited to the following requirements:

a. Satisfy all responsibilities as outlined in reference (b).

b. Develop and maintain a (COMMAND) IA program that identifies IA architecture; IA requirements; IA objectives and policies; IA personnel; and IA processes and procedures.

c. Provide security oversight for (COMMAND) and subordinate commands. This includes coordinating (COMMAND) security measures including analysis, periodic testing, evaluation, verification, accreditation, and review of information system installations.

d. Ensure information ownership responsibilities are established for each (COMMAND) information system, to include accountability, access approvals, and special handling requirements.

e. Ensure the development, review, endorsement, and maintenance of IA certification and accreditation documentation, in accordance with reference (i). A repository of this documentation and all modifications should be maintained.

f. Ensure IA Officers (IAOs) are appointed in writing, to include their assigned duties and responsibilities identified in reference (d). All IAOs are also required to receive the necessary technical or management and IA training, education, and certifications required to carry out their respective duties.

g. Ensure compliance monitoring occurs, and review the results of such monitoring, notifying the DAA of significant, i.e., CAT I findings.

h. Coordinate security measures to include analysis, periodic testing, evaluation, verification, and review of information system installation at the appropriate classification level within the command or organizational network structure.

i. Develop reporting procedures and ensure security violations and incidents are properly reported to the Computer Network Defense Service Provider (CNDSP), Navy Cyber Defense Operations Command (NCDOC), and the DoD reporting chain, as required.

j. Ensure procedures are developed and implemented in accordance with configuration management (CM) policies and practices for authorizing the use of software on information systems.

k. Serve as a member of the CM board or delegate this responsibility to the properly appointed command Information Assurance Officer (IAO).

l. Ensure users and system support personnel have the required background investigation, security clearance, authorization, and need-to-know and are indoctrinated on (COMMAND) security practices before granting access to information systems.

m. Ensure audit trails (system logs) are reviewed periodically and audit records are archived and maintained for future reference.

n. Ensure system users are provided initial and annual IA awareness training, and system administrator, management, and network security personnel are provided appropriate systems security training for their duties.

o. Ensure completion of training and certifications for command IA Workforce personnel are up to date in the Information Assurance Workforce Management Tool.

4. You are to provide your contact information to the Regional IAM who maintains the list of IAMs.

5. This appointment is effective until rescinded in writing.

> First Last
> Commander/Commanding Officer <or
> By direction>

Copy to:
EII/GNOC Detachment Regional IAM or MSC/MCNOSC IAM

APPENDIX D - DEFINITIONS

A-76 - Office of Management and Budget (OMB) Circular A-76 establishes Federal policy regarding the performance of commercial activities. Circular A-76 sets forth the procedures for determining whether commercial activities should be performed under contract with commercial sources or in-house using Government facilities and personnel.

Basic Skill - A developed capacity that facilitates learning or the more rapid acquisition of new knowledge, or facilitates conveying information to others.

Community Management - Encompasses all processes required to shape the workforce to meet the service mission. Includes recruiting goals, retention monitoring, re-enlistment incentives, advancement/career progression, rotation policy and transfer to Fleet Reserve/retirement authority. IAWF Management encompasses officers, enlisted, and civilians that may be in other functional communities.

Competency - Competencies are measurable knowledge, skills, abilities, behaviors and other characteristics an individual needs to perform a particular job or job function successfully.

Computing Environment (CE) - Per reference (j), local area network (s) server host and its operating system, peripherals, and applications.

Cybersecurity Workforce (CSWF) - This term is used interchangeably with Information Assurance Workforce. Cybersecurity is defined as, "Prevention of damage to, protection of, and restoration of computers, electronic communications systems, electronic communications services, wire communication, and electronic communications, including information contained therein, to ensure its availability, integrity, authentication, confidentially and non-repudiation." (NPSPD 54/HSPD 23)

Cyberspace (CS) - a global domain within the information environment consisting of the interdependent network of information technology infrastructures, including the Internet, telecommunications networks, computer systems, and embedded processors and controllers.

-

Defense Civilian Personnel Data System (DCPDS) - DCPDS is the mandatory DOD-wide system for processing civilian personnel actions and retaining personnel data. It hosts both position and person data elements and feeds the civilian pay data system.

Distance Support - The combination of process and technology to provide the effective transfer of information that improves the productivity of the Sailor and Marine while deployed.

Distribution - Allocation of personnel to billets. The manpower requirements process establishes the job requirements for billets. The distributions process matches individuals with the requisite skills to specific billets.

Enclave - As defined in Reference (j) a collection of CE connected by one or more internal networks under the control of a single authority and security policy, including personnel and physical security. Enclaves provide standard IA capabilities such as boundary defense, incident detection and response, and key management, and also deliver common applications such as office automation and electronic mail. Enclaves are analogous to general support systems, as defined in OMB A-130 at reference (g). Enclaves may be specific to an organization or a mission and the CE may be organized by physical proximity or by function, independent of location. Examples of enclaves include local area networks and the applications they host, backbone networks, and data processing centers.

Foreign National - Individuals who are non-U.S. citizens including U.S. military personnel, DoD civilian employees, and contractors.

Human Capital - The knowledge, skills, abilities and capacities possessed by people. Human capital can be acquired in many ways, including education, on-the-job training, experience, employment opportunities, etc. The capability, capacity, creativity, etc. possessed by individuals.

Information Assurance - Measures that protect and defend information and ISs by ensuring their availability, integrity, authentication, confidentiality, and non-repudiation. Per reference (d) these measures include providing for restoration of IS by incorporating protection, detection, and reaction capabilities.

Information Assurance Workforce - The IAWF focuses on the operation and management of IA capabilities for DoD systems and networks. The workforce ensures adequate security measures and established IA policies and procedures are applied to all ISs and networks. The IAWF includes anyone with privileged access, system architects, system engineers, computer network defense service providers, Certifying Agents and their subordinates, Red Team, Blue Teams, and IA managers who perform any of the responsibilities or functions described in reference (b). These individuals are considered to have significant "security responsibilities" and must receive specialized training and be reported per Reference (b) and (c).

Joint Capabilities Integration and Development System (JCIDS) - JCIDS is a joint concepts-centric capabilities identification process that allows joint forces to meet future military challenges. The full range of doctrine, organization, training, materiel, leadership and education, personnel and facilities (DOTMLPF) solutions.

Marine Corps Enterprise Network - The MCEN includes all Marine Corps voice and data networks and ISs including wired or wireless, in garrison or deployed, that process, store, and/or transmit Marine Corps information.

National Security Personnel System (NSPS) - The National Defense Authorization Act for Fiscal Year 2004 gives the DoD the authority to establish a more flexible civilian personnel management system - the National Security Personnel System (NSPS).

Network Environment (Computer) - The constituent element of an enclave responsible for connecting CE by providing short haul data transport capabilities, such as local or campus area networks, or long haul data transport capabilities, such as operational, metropolitan, or wide area and backbone networks that provides for the application of IA controls.

Pay for Performance - The concept in the NSPS Performance Management system that compensates employees based on performance in support of the organization's mission.

Performance Standard - The measurable demonstrated behavior required to complete a task.

Privileged Access. An authorized user who has access to system control, monitoring, administration, criminal investigation, or compliance functions. Privileged access typically provides access to the following system controls:

- Access to the control functions of the IS/network, administration of user accounts, etc.
- Access to change control parameters (e.g., routing tables, path priorities, addresses) of routers, multiplexers, and other key IS/network equipment or software.
- Ability and authority to control and change program files, and other users' access to data.
- Direct access to OS level functions that permit system controls to be bypassed or changed.
- Access and authority for installing, configuring, monitoring security monitoring functions of information systems/networks (e.g., network/system analyzers; intrusion detection software; firewalls) or in performance of cyber/network defense operations.

Professional Military Education (PME) - Progressive levels of military education that prepares military officers for leadership. It includes basic level courses for new and junior officers, command and staff colleges for mid-level officers and war colleges for senior officers.

Proficiency - Ability to perform a specific behavior (e.g., task, learning objective) to the established performance standard in order to demonstrate mastery of the behavior.

Readiness Analysis - Readiness Analysis is direct comparison of required proficiency levels of the work against the rated proficiency levels of the persons performing the work.

Total Force - All personnel assets, active and reserve military, government civilian and contractor.

Training Continuum - The Sailor's Training Continuum and Marine Corps Career Roadmap are tools to ensure mission accomplishment and provide opportunities to grow professionally and personally. Both service tools map and measure an individual's career progress and identifies learning resources that lead to achieving career milestones.

Un-supervised Privileged Access - When a member of the IAWF arrives from initial training and is able to access SYSADMIN functions without having a qualified IAT present to provide OJT. To gain privileged access the member should hold the appropriate commercial certification and be supervised for around a six month time period. OJT applies only to IAT level I environment.

APPENDIX E - ABBREVIATIONS AND/OR ACRONYMS

Acronym	Meaning
ASD NII/DoD CIO	Assistant Secretary of Defense for Networks and Information Integration/ DoD Chief Information Officer
CA	Certifying Authority
C&A	Certification and Accreditation
CAR	Certifying Authority Representative
CBT	Computer Based Training
CE	Computing Environment
CIO	Command Information Officer
CND SP	Computer Network Defense Service Provider
CNSS	Committee on National Security Systems
DAA	Designated Accrediting Authority
DCPDS	Defense Civilian Personnel Data System
DIAP	Defense Information Assurance Office
DISA	Defense Information Systems Agency
DMDC	Defense Manpower Data Center
DoD	Department of Defense
DON CIO	Department of the Navy Chief Information Officer
EII	Navy Echelon II
FISMA	Federal Information Security Management Act
FN	Foreign National
GIG	Global Information Grid
IA	Information Assurance
IAM Levels I-III	Information Assurance Management levels I-III
IAM	Information Assurance Manager
IAT Levels I-III	Information Assurance Technical levels I-III
IASAE	Information Assurance System Architect and Engineer
IAWF	Information Assurance Workforce

Acronym	Meaning
IA WIP	Information Assurance Workforce Improvement Program
INFOSEC	Information Systems Security (The parenthetical title in DCPDS for civilian personnel performing IA functions)
IS	Information System
IT	Information Technology
LN	Local National
MSC	Marine Corps Major Subordinate Command
NACI	National Agency Check with written Inquiries
NE	Network Environment
OJT	On the Job Training
OS	Operating System
PSC	Position Specialty Code
SSBI	Single Scope Background Investigation
SYSADMIN	System Administrator
TF	Total Force
TWMS	Total Workforce Management System
USD (P&R)	Under Secretary of Defense for Personnel and Readiness
WIPAC	ASD NII/ DoD CIO and USD P&R Information Assurance Workforce Improvement Advisory Council

APPENDIX F - IA WORKFORCE DETERMINATION

<table>
<tr><td colspan="2" align="center"><Command Name>
Information Assurance Workforce Assessment
Questionnaire</td></tr>
<tr><td>Name</td><td>Email Address</td></tr>
<tr><td>Compa
ny</td><td>Phone</td></tr>
<tr><td colspan="2" align="center">Questions – Please respond to the questions below by checking the appropriate response:</td></tr>
</table>

QUESTION - Must answer more than one question to be part of the workforce.	YES/NO	
1. Do you have an End User Agreement (EUA), DD Form 2875 modified 12 June 2006, on file with the Command IAM / Alternate IAM?	☐ Yes	☐ No
2. Do you log on with a systems administrator account on a Government system?	☐ Yes	☐ No
3. Do you create user accounts or modify user permissions or roles for other users on a Government application, workstation, server, or network?	☐ Yes	☐ No
4. Do you have the permissions and capability to install software on a Government server, workstation, or network device?	☐ Yes	☐ No
5. Do you manage or otherwise have permissions to modify network devices for Government networks?	☐ Yes	☐ No
6. Do you have the permissions and capability to install hardware on Government computer systems?	☐ Yes	☐ No
7. Do you have the permissions and capability to install peripherals on Government computer systems?	☐ Yes	☐ No
8. Do you have permissions to access and/or modify a database for a Government owned application on a Government computer system?	☐ Yes	☐ No
9. Do you have the capability to delete or otherwise modify user accounts on Government systems?	☐ Yes	☐ No
10. Are you responsible for maintenance, repair, or related upkeep of Government-owned computer or IT-related hardware at your site or installation?	☐ Yes	☐ No
11. Can you perform system upgrades or modifications on Government computer systems?	☐ Yes	☐ No
12. Can you perform network scans (e.g., ISS, RETINA) on Government computer systems?	☐ Yes	☐ No
13. Can you perform surveillance or monitoring on Government computer systems?	☐ Yes	☐ No
14. Do you move, install, or uninstall Government computer systems?	☐ Yes	☐ No
15. Do you create, initiate, or otherwise enact system, database, or application backup or restoration activities on Government owned application, workstation, server, or network?	☐ Yes	☐ No
16. Are you an integral part of the design process or the development of IA Systems?	☐ Yes	☐ No
17. Are you a Computer Network Defense Service Provider?	☐ Yes	☐ No
18. Are you a member of the Red Team, Blue Team, or C& A Team ?	☐ Yes	☐ No
18. Are you a 27XX NEC in the Navy? Are you an 06XX MOS in the Marine Corps?	☐ Yes	☐ No
19. Are you a 16XX Designator in the Navy? Are you an 06XX MOS in the Marine Corps?	☐ Yes	☐ No

APPENDIX G – OS COMMERCIAL CERTIFICATION GUIDANCE

Certification (# = Required)	IAT-I			IAT-II				IAT-III			
	Desktop Support	Network Infra-structure	Domain Infra-structure	Network Infra-structure	Data-base Support	Web Ser-vice	Domain Infra-structure	Network Infra-structure	Data-base Sup-port	Web Ser-vice	Soft-ware Devel-oper
MCDST (WXP)	X										
MCITP-EST (Vista)	X										
MCP-WXP	X										
#70-270											
MCP-W2K Pro*	X										
#70-210											
MCP-WNT WS*	X										
#70-073											
Solaris SCSA	X		X		X	X			X	X	X
LPIC1	X										
Linux+	X		X		X	X			X	X	X
RHCT	X										
HP CSA	X		X		X	X			X	X	X
CCENT		X		X							
CWNA		X									
MCSA (W2K*/W2K3)			X		X	X			X	X	X
MCITP-SA (W2K8)			X		X	X			X	X	X
MCP-W2K Srvr*			X		X	X			X	X	X
#70-215											
#70-216											
#70-217											
MCP-W2K3			X		X	X			X	X	X
#70-290											
#70-291											
#70-299											
MCP-WNT Srvr*			X								
#70-067											
#70-068											
RHCE			X		X	X			X	X	X
LPIC2			X		X	X					
Server+					X	X					
CCNA				X							
CAWLFS				X							
CWSP				X							

Certification (# = Required)	IAT-I			IAT-II				IAT-III			
	Desktop Support	Network Infra-structure	Domain Infra-structure	Network Infra-structure	Data-base Support	Web Ser-vice	Domain Infra-structure	Network Infra-structure	Data-base Sup-port	Web Ser-vice	Soft-ware Devel-oper
CIW-A						X**					
CIW-P										X**	
MCTS-SQL2K5					X**						
MCTS-SQL2K8					X**						
DBA OCA					X**						
SYBASE ASAA					X**				X**		
SYBASE ASAP									X**		
MCSE (W2K*/W2K3)							X				
MCITP-EA (W2K8)							X				
Solaris SCNA							X				
HP CSE							X				
RHCDS							X				
LPIC3							X		X	X	X
CCNP								X			
CCDE								X			
CAWLDS								X			
CWNE								X			
CIW-MA										X**	
CSDP											X**
DBA OCP									X**		
DBA OCM									X**		
Fleet Training Tools											
Juniper Networks IDS					X				X		
CND OSE											

* Certification exams/tracks are no longer offered but are still valid and will be required to support such Computing Environments.

** Highly recommend coupling with a server-based certification

Commanding Officers determine the appropriate OS/CE certification/s

APPENDIX H - IA WORKFORCE MANAGEMENT REVIEW CHECKLIST

DON Information Assurance Workforce Management Inspection Checklist	
Critical Element	Have IA and HR management personnel at the site level developed and implemented IA Workforce Improvement Program (IA WIP)?
Purpose	To assess the capability, performance and compliance against the policies and requirements of DoDD 8570.1 and DoD 8570.01-M.
Core Review Areas	IA Workforce Management, IA Training, IA Certification
Method	Review of IA WIP program plans, including documentation and procedures review.

	YES	NO	N/A	Source	Comment
A. IA Workforce Management					
1. Is the CO familiar with 8570.01-M IA WIP and FISMA requirements?				C.O./IAM	
2. Have the DoD 8570.01-M and DON IA WIP Plans been distributed to the IAWF?				C.O., N/G6, IAWF	
3. Has the site developed and implemented its own IA WIP policy/guidance?				IAM; Personnel Officer	
4. Are all IA positions with IA functions identified by category and level in the site's manpower tables of organization? *(DoD 8570.01-M, Chapter 7, para C7.2.2)*				DCPDS; TWMS; TFFMS; MCTFS;	
5. Are the DON CIO, CNO N6, HQMC C4 and NNWC official messages on IAWF Management accessible?				Admin; official websites	
6. # of IA Positions _identified_ by category/level in the personnel and staffing database(s) *(DoD 8570.01-M, Chapter 8, para 8.2.7.1.2)*				DCPDS; TWMS; MCTIMS;	
7. # of IA positions _filled_ by category and level in the personnel and staffing database(s) *(DoD 8570.01-M, Chapter 8, para 8.2.7.1.5)*				DCPDS; TWMS; MCTIMS;	
8. Are all positions and personnel with IA responsibilities identified in the appropriate database, regardless of occupational specialty?				DCPDS; TWMS;MCTIMS;	
9. Are these individuals further identified as performing IA responsibilities as primary or as an additional, or embedded duty? *(DoD 8570.01-M, Chapter 8,*				DCPDS; TWMS; MCTIMS;	

paras C8.2.7.1.3 & C8.2.7.1.4)					
10. Is training available for HR personnel on the systems/processes required to support the IA WIP manpower and personnel management requirements?				Local Training Records; electronic Training Jacket	
11. Have all IA personnel with privileged access completed a "Privileged Access Agreement?" Show examples.				Local Official Files; TWMS	
12. Do all IA personnel with privileged access have a Common Access Card (CAC) to control access?				IAWF	
13. # of users who completed the IA orientation/awareness annual training requirement versus total number of authorized users *(DoD 8570.01-M, Chapter 8, para C8.2.7.4)*				Electronic training jacket; NTMPS; MarineNet	
B. IA Training					
1. Does the site have an official IA Training Plan and is it implemented?				Official Site Training Plan	
2. Does the training plan state specialized training necessary (i.e. HBSS for privileged access users performing IA functions)?				Official Site Training Plan	
3. How many of those with privileged access responsibilities have received the required training.				IAWF Members	
4. What is the timeline for training the remaining individuals identified with significant security responsibilities to receive specialized training?				Local IA Training or Implementation Plan	
5. What are the reasons for all identified personnel not having yet received specialized training (i.e. insufficient funding, insufficient time, courses unavailable, personnel are not registered)?				Commanding Officer, IAM, and IAWF	
6. Are detailed training records maintained for all IA personnel? (records that indicate the exact training for each member)				Local Training Records;	
7. Does the site have on the job training (OJT) for newly assigned IAMs and personnel with privileged access?				Local IA WIP Implementation Plan	
8. Is an oversight structure in place that manages the IA training				Commanding Officer; Local IA WIP	

program? Is there documentation of IA training oversight structure to include Training Officers and supervisors of IAM, personnel with privileged access, CND, IASAE, C&A and all IA professionals?				Implementation Plan/Training Plan	
10. #/% of personnel with privileged access who have documented completion of the OJT requirement.				Local Official Records; Training Officer	
11. Are plans for continued learning a part of the training plan?				IA WIP Plan Electronic support	
12. #/% of personnel with privileged access, IAMs, CND, IASAE, C&A and DAA completing continuing training requirements.				Training Database; Local Training Records; IAWF	
13. Have all assigned DAAs completed the DoD DAA training within 60 days of assignment (or the NDU/IRMC CNSSI No. 4012 course/certificate) or equivalent training? *(DoD 8570.01-M, Chapter 5, paras C5.3.1.1 and C5.3.2)*				Local Training Records; Training Database	
14. Are course completion certificates available for DAA? *(DoD 8570.01-M, para C5.3.1.3)*				Local Official Records	
C. IA Certification Program					
1. Does the site have a plan that establishes timelines and procedures for all current and new IA personnel to be appropriately certified for their primary position?				C.O.; Training Officer; Local IA WIP Implementation Plan	
2. What is the oversight process in place to ensure all site contracts include contractor compliance requirements? (DFARS 48 CFR Parts 239 and 252 RIN 0750-AF 52 DFARS: IA Contractor Training and Certification (DFARS Case 2006-D023)				C.O.; Acquisition and Budget Personnel; Electronic Databases; IAM, IAWF	
3. Has the site identified appropriate "operating system certification" requirements and trained their workforce with privileged access?				C.O.; Supervisors	
4. Is an oversight process in place that ensures all incumbents and new hires are trained, certified and recertified?				C.O.; IAM, IAWF	

STOCK NUMBER
0516LP1102790